To Glen –

Temple of the Soul

Real Life ER Stories from Las Vegas.

D0889221

By

Marsha Oritt, M.S.W.

Edited By Julie B. Gallai, R.N., B.S.N.

Marsha Oritt
8/03

COPYRIGHT © 2002 BY MARSHA ORITT

ALL RIGHTS RESERVED. ANY PART OF THIS BOOK
MAY BE REPRODUCED IN ANY FORM OR BY ANY
ELECTRONIC OR MECHANICAL MEANS, INCLUDING
INFORMATION STORAGE, AND RETRIEVAL SYSTEMS,
AS LONG AS THE WORK IS CREDITED TO TEMPLE
OF THE SOUL BY MARSHA ORITT.

First Edition # 886388
Writers Guild of America, Incorporated
Intellectual Property Registry
7000 West Third Street
Los Angeles, California 90048-4329

ISBN 0-9726043-0-8
First Printing   (December 2002)

Additional Copies of this book are available by mail at:
M.L.O. Enterprises
2800 Autumn Haze Lane
Las Vegas, Nevada 89117
Fax (702) 804-0569
E-mail: marshaoritt@lvcm.com

Printed in the U.S.A by
Western Typesetters, Inc.

TESTIMONIALS

"One woman's journey into the world of hospital emergency services... written from the heart."
—Chris Melendez, Security Officer

"Educational, inspirational & thought provoking!"
—Brooke Nicolls, High School Teacher

"Easy to understand, written for the lay person."
—Rosalie Feffer, Home Health Care Worker

"Totally new perspective on medical care. Human interest stories that grab you by your heart strings."
—Laurie Dressler, Computer Programmer

"Down-to-earth... Raw with emotions, action packed..."
—Kathleen Marco, Drug & Alcohol Counselor

DISCLAIMER

This book does not give medical advice. Always consult your doctor and other professionals. The ideas and suggestions contained in this book are not intended to be a substitute for consulting with a physician.

All matters regarding your health require medical supervision.

The names of all those who contributed anecdotal materials in this book have been changed to respect their privacy.

DEDICATION

I wish to express my deepest appreciation to nurses worldwide. They are the backbone of every health care system. Though under-appreciated, underpaid, and overworked, we could not survive without them.

ACKNOWLEDGEMENTS

This author is indebted to many fine people for their assistance in helping put this book together. Special thanks to the following:

Dr. Joseph Fayad, who saw me through the most difficult challenge of my life. His unwavering belief in his ability to "cure" my illness and his kindness and support rekindled my desire to work in emergency medicine services.

My supervisor, Alice Conroy, Director of the Emergency Department at Sunrise Hospital, for giving me the opportunity to learn, to grow, and to enrich my life in ways I had never imagined.

To the wonderful nurses at Sunrise Hospital who go to work every day and face monumental tasks with patience and compassion. I am proud to work beside every one of them.

To the emergency medical technicians for rushing to the aid of the sick and injured often risking their own lives and never forgetting that every minute can make the difference between life and death.

To Oprah Winfrey and her "Angel Network" for motivating me to "make a difference" with my life.

To my mentor, Dr. Phil McGraw, for inspiring me to "tell it like it is." His advice and direct approach has been an invaluable resource to me and, indirectly, to all my patients.

To my best friend and next-door-neighbor Corey Buskey, who has always believed in my ability to turn this time period into book form.

To Ernie, my dog, for providing me with much-needed kisses and affection when I dragged myself home in the wee hours of the morning.

Special thanks to the thousands of patients who have passed through the emergency department this past year. Many have touched my soul in ways I had never known and will not forget.

CONTENTS

PROLOGUE

The emergency department was busier than usual today. I arrived at work to find five ambulances parked in front of the staff entrance. I took a deep breath, grounded myself, and walked through the door. There were ten paramedics calmly waiting in the hall outside the triage office, patients in tow. They brought in a drug overdose, three heart attacks, and a stroke victim. Each patient was equipped with intravenous tubing and oxygen masks.

The waiting room was packed, every seat taken. The air conditioner was not working adequately and it was hot and sticky. Waiting time would be hours today and the patients were becoming crabby and restless. They were all experiencing various degrees of pain and discomfort. One person appeared to be passing a kidney stone, another was badly beaten. All this suffering and it wasn't even noon yet.

By early evening the crowd was even larger. One young pregnant woman arrived with severe abdominal pain and bleeding. Others were suffering from chest pains, migraines, and broken bones. Within the hour the paramedics returned with more sick and injured, all needing immediate medical intervention. The local news program just showed pictures of a major car pile-up on Highway 95. Nothing unusual about that. After all, this is Las Vegas- the fastest growing city in America.

INTRODUCTION

I moved to Las Vegas in the summer of 1998. Why? Like most, I was looking for a new start, low humidity, employment opportunities, and new friends. I had no idea what joy was waiting for me.

This book originated from a journal I began the day I went to work as a social worker in the emergency room of the largest hospital in Las Vegas. There were so many new sights, smells, emotions, and experiences. I was overwhelmed by my feelings and at times I thought my heart would just break. Invariably, I was challenged on every level of my being. I witnessed so much pain and suffering, but also tremendous compassion and joy, and of course... death.

Prior to this job, I had given little thought to the meaning of death; my own or others'. A few close relatives had passed away in recent years and I have had some personal crisis that brought it home to me but the thoughts were fleeting and their long-term impact were negligible. I had not seriously questioned my ideas and beliefs about a "higher power" or the "here-after" either.

I had maintained private diaries intermittently through-out my life, especially when feeling overwhelmed or depressed. Writing had always enabled me to gain insight and work through whatever issues were surfacing at the time.

It had been a few years since the last journal entry but I knew it was time to begin again. I had completed my first twelve hour shift at the hospital and it was 4:00 in the morning. I had been tossing and turning in bed for three hours, rehashing all of the events of the day. My mind simply refused to quiet down. Suddenly an inner voice beckoned me to get up. Without a second thought, I raced downstairs, grabbed a pen and a tablet, and proceeded to put all my thoughts and feelings down on paper.

Two hours and ten pages of scribble later, my mind was cleansed enough to return to bed. I fell asleep immediately with imagined ideas of what the second day had in store for me. At best, I would face it with only four hours of shut-eye.

I spent many sleepless nights documenting what occurred during those emotionally driven days. I desperately needed to grasp all that was happening around me. My mind was like a dry sponge. I was overwhelmed by this new world I had plunged into but had never felt so alive.

My purpose here is to share some of the highlights and to help you through the emergency room experience so you will be better prepared when you come to a hospital as a patient.

1

LIFE CRISIS HITS HOME

A short time after arriving in Las Vegas, I re-opened both my private investigation and financial planning businesses. Three months later I had some lab work done and was informed that the Hepatitis C I had contracted back in 1968, had escalated into a life threatening condition. My liver enzymes, which measure how effectively the liver is functioning, were escalating way beyond the normal range. This was a clear indication that my liver was not working well. I agreed to have a liver biopsy performed. A biopsy is the only precise method to determine the extent of the damage. The results were devastating. I was diagnosed with cirrhosis, stage four; the most critical of the four stages of this disease. Unless something was done quickly, I would be facing liver failure, a high probability of liver cancer, and quite possibly, a liver transplant in my future. In the United States, there are currently more than sixty thousand people on transplant waiting lists. Only seventeen thousand organs are available. The odds of getting a transplant are slim at best, and the cost can be $350,000 and higher. I needed another option. My doctor recommended a regime of experimental drugs in massive quantities to attempt to destroy the virus. If the virus was destroyed, my liver would most likely function at a higher level and the deterioration might be slowed down or even stopped.

With the help and support of my liver doctor and with blind faith, I decided that if I wanted to live a healthy and productive life, I should just "go for it". He made me fully aware that at that time, the "success" rate was twenty to fifty percent and the odds of it working for me were much lower due to the cirrhosis. He added that this was a new treatment and it had not been tested for long-term effects. Though terrified, I realized that if I wanted to live much longer, I had no choice. I expected to feel sick but I had no idea the impact that year would have on every area of my life.

A miracle happened within the first thirty days of treatment: The hepatitis C virus was no longer detectable in my blood. I was ecstatic. I had to remain on this regime for a year to give myself the best possible opportunity of prolonged success. I spent the year injecting myself with interferon three times a week and daily I ingested three capsules of ribavirin, a chemical that has antiviral activity designed to accentuate the effects of the interferon. Since this combination was created to "destroy" the hepatitis C virus, the side effects were horrific. The enclosed literature alluded to sixty possible side effects as "flu-like symptoms." Not true! I experienced at least seventy-five side effects and no flu could come close to what I was feeling. I became anemic, suffered from acid-reflux, hair loss, insomnia, and lost forty-five pounds. All foods tasted metallic and caused intense heart-burn. My body would only tolerate oatmeal and that is what I ate for breakfast, lunch, and dinner. My eyesight changed constantly and I had to get two new sets of glasses. My mind was so fuzzy that I couldn't concentrate and I got lost every time I left home. My entire body seemed to be malfunctioning. I could barely walk or speak. When I did attempt to talk, I made little sense. My depth perception was so poor that I fell down stairs and slammed into walls constantly.

Many days I laid in bed, only getting up to use the bathroom and feed my dog, Ernie. I was so sick that I did not expect to live through the treatment.

Needless to say, I had plenty of time for personal reflection. During those long, horrible months, I dissected my past with intense scrutiny and honesty. I made amends to others and promised myself that if I had a future, I would get back into social work and help others.

Within a week of stopping treatment, I began to feel like my old self again. My appetite returned, the "brain fog" cleared and I began to wake up happy. I stopped reacting to life's minor "complications" and focused on the positive things around me. I had been transformed into a better person.

Six months passed quickly and I remained virus-free. I was getting stronger every day. I was ready to get my life back on track and I wanted a job that would allow me the opportunity to "be there" for others going through medical calamities. I applied for the social worker position at the local hospital and was hired. I was ecstatic! I would finally utilize my master's degree in medical social work and keep the promise I had made to myself. As it turned out, I would be able to fulfill this goal in more ways than I could have imagined.

The following stories are some of the highlights of that first year. I interacted with thousands of patients during that time period. These are just a few of the many who made a significant impact on me. The people are all real but the names have been changed to ensure their privacy.

2

FIRST DAY JITTERS

Will It Be Like The TV Show?

I awoke with a flood of emotions on top of the usual first day jitters. I understood that my new job would be emotionally and intellectually challenging. I was preoccupied with thoughts of blood, vomit, injuries, and death."Could I handle it?" I wondered. I was too nervous to eat breakfast so I settled for a slice of whole-wheat toast with a little margarine, showered, and got dressed. I carefully selected a nice pair of dress slacks, sweater, and sneakers, and topped the outfit off with a white lab coat that I had specially ordered with my name embroidered in script with royal blue thread. My heart raced with anticipation.

Summer arrived with a vengeance, making the air stifling, arid, and unrelenting in its abuse. Since I have lived here for a few years, I already knew that the forces of nature would engulf the city for the next four months. I ignored the weather and instead focused on my feelings of apprehension and excitement while I walked outside to my car.

My thoughts were interrupted when a scorching burst of hot wind whipped through me like a furnace blast from the depths of Hell. It was already 106 degrees and it was only 9:30 in the morning. The swirling gusts of dry heat almost knocked me to the ground. The air here can be quite oppressive and that makes it especially difficult to function in any normal capacity.

I started up my electric-blue, 1994 Miata convertible. The motor groaned and sputtered as the air conditioner struggled to cool me off. During my twenty minute commute to work, I passed all types of cars, SUVs, mini-vans, motor homes, and campers registered from every state in the country. Thirty-five million people come here yearly to try to win what they are not able to earn. The allure of instant wealth is the city's calling card and the "party town" illusion is everywhere. Fifteen minutes later, I passed the famous "Las Vegas Strip." It is a wondrous sight. Mammoth casinos present a faux vision of the world at large, re-creating miniature versions of other cities such as New York, Venice and Paris. Millions of dollars are spent to lure tourists into the belief that the city can transport them into never-never land. Only in Las Vegas can you see pirate ships, volcanoes, pyramids, gondolas, even the Eiffel Tower, all within a two-mile radius.

Once past the Strip, Las Vegas is like any other city. Suburban homes ooze across the horizon with their tiny yards covered with imported grasses and trees. There are strip malls every few blocks scarring the landscape. Residents speak about living on the East side or West side, in Green Valley, The Lakes, Summerlin or downtown but the city looks basically the same everywhere.

The people who call Las Vegas home are an eclectic mix of senior citizens, baby boomers, unskilled laborers, and young adults, not unlike most cities except for the large numbers. Las Vegas has a low unemployment rate with a high demand for workers in the construction and service industries. Housing is less expensive than in most states and there are no state income taxes. The humidity remains low, which seems to reduce the pains of arthritis and muscular ailments, and the sun shines brightly more than ninety-five percent of the year. It is a great place to live, especially for those who are financially secure and healthy.

Las Vegas is where dreams are supposed to come true. But, when things go wrong, and life suddenly goes awry, you might meet me at my place of employment.

By the time I arrived to work, I was already exhausted from all these concerns but at the same time; I was exhilarated with thoughts of what may lie ahead.

I pulled into the beige six-story employee parking garage and searched for a spot. As soon as I again hit daylight, I noticed six ambulances lined up outside the entrance. The sign was bright neon fluorescent orange; the letters read "Ambulances Only." As I walked up to the entrance I nodded hello to everyone standing outside, held my identification card up to the little black box on the wall and waited for the beep and the green light to flash. The doors magically parted - beckoning me forward. By this point, my mind was racing with anticipation.

Right inside the door were six patients experiencing varying degrees of pain. They were all lying on gurneys and had intravenous lines with fluids dripping into their arms. Two of them had oxygen masks covering their noses and mouths. The paramedics hovered over them possessively. I said hi to them and kept walking. I was afraid to look too closely and did not want to stare. The hallway to my new office seemed to stretch on for a mile.

I knocked on the door, walked in, and introduced myself to my new office mates. A large, friendly, gregarious woman immediately stood up and introduced herself as Caroline. Up until today, she had been the only social worker assigned to the adult section of the emergency room and she made me feel comfortable immediately. She was very happy that I was coming on board and would be "holding down the fort" when she was off-duty. She was easy to talk to and I felt an instant "kinship" with her. Caroline informed me that I would only get three days of orientation with her by my side. The panic I felt must have shown on my face as she quickly added that she would be happy to leave her pager and cell phone on for the next month so I could reach her at any time. In just three short days, I would be the only mental health counselor for the entire adult emergency department during my twelve hour shift. I gulped and took a very deep breath.

Caroline escorted me to the staff lounge and showed me where to slide my identification badge through the time card machine. Thus began my tour.

The Emergency Department

We walked down another very long hallway. Caroline held her badge up to a different black box and the doors flung open. We again passed by the paramedics who were still waiting in the hall, and proceeded to the triage area.

Before a patient can be seen by a nurse, he must fill out a half-sheet of paper with the name, address, and present complaint. He/she is called into the triage office where a nurse takes his blood pressure and temperature. The patient informs the nurse about his complaint and symptoms. Patients are always seen according to the severity of their conditions, NOT when they arrive. After spending a few minutes observing, we left the triage office and headed for the treatment areas.

This section of the emergency department was newly

renovated and it was light and clean. The walls were painted shades of teal which gave off a sense of peacefulness. The air held faint traces of urine and feces. I wondered why there was no telltale smells of the "medicinal odor" I had remembered from an early childhood tonsillectomy.

The emergency department is divided into three main sections. Rooms one through sixteen make up the critical care area. These beds are reserved for those suffering from chest pains, shortness of breath, are on ventilators or in comas. The patients are placed there if they are at serious risk of death. Referred to as Station One, it is centrally located and is the "hub" of the ER. The doctors congregate in this area so the patients can be closely monitored and administered treatment on a moment's notice. The rooms are crowded and confining. Only curtains separate those suffering varying degrees of trauma and sickness. One with minor chest pains may be sharing a room with another who is in a coma and near death. No thought is given to the sex of the patient; Assignments are done strictly by the presenting medical needs.

Rooms seven, eight, and nine in Station One provide the

best visual access. They are much more spacious than the other thirteen in the section to accommodate additional equipment and staff in the event of a "code." This is the medical vernacular used when a patient stops breathing or his heart ceases beating. I consider these three our "bad luck" rooms as they seem to have more deaths occur in them than the other rooms in this section.

The treatment areas form a circle. Station Two is further down the hall. Each room has a door, a color television, and only one bed. They are most commonly used for those suffering from abdominal pain, migraines, kidney stones, and female problems of all types.

The patients in Station Three have a conglomerate of illnesses and problems. The employees refer to this area as "skid row" because the rooms are most often filled with men and women who are intoxicated, drug addicted, mentally ill, or homeless.

Security officers are assigned to the ones who may be violent, suicidal, or have a legal hold placed on them. Any suicidal gesture or proclamations of suicide result in a Legal 2000 form being issued by a police officer, a nurse, doctor, or social worker to prevent a patient from leaving the hospital for at least seventy-two hours. During that time period, a counselor from an outside mental health agency is sent in to assess the patient. The counselor then determines whether the patient can be discharged home or will be sent on to one of the two main mental health hospitals in town for further evaluation and treatment. Nevada has the nation's highest suicide rate and any gestures or verbal proclamations are taken very seriously.

During those early months, I constantly re-lived events. My high moments were exhilarating but short-lived; I ruminated on my "mistakes" for hours, especially at bedtime when my dreams were filled with reenactments of the previous day. I felt like a fish out of water - a real neophyte in this strange new world. Everything was unfamiliar; even the language was foreign. Though nervous and insecure, I enjoyed every minute of my day and was confident that I could handle the job. I was pushed, pulled, molded and challenged on every level. I had no idea that I would witness so much death, pain, loss, miracles and love. My "heart" was getting quite a work-out. Though nervous and insecure, I was confident that I could handle whatever was thrown at me. I discovered that I had an unlimited ability to handle frustration, compassion, and fear, both my own and those of my patients. My sense of purpose would be permanently transformed along with my ideas about spirituality, the meaning of life, and the concept of death.

No two days are ever the same in the emergency department. People from all walks of life and from every corner of the globe pass through our doors. Every one is unique but there is a common thread that we all share... the need for compassion and understanding.

A New Day

I just arrived at work. It is early in the day and there are already five emergency vehicles lined up right outside the ambulance entrance to the hospital. Some are yellow, red, white, and blue; others are white and blue but they all have "911' in large letters and the medical symbol printed on either side. The scene reminds me of the long taxi lines outside the major casinos on the strip. Whew! So busy already? It's going to be one of those days.

"Hi Luella!" I called out as I waved to the monitor of the waiting room. Luella is a sturdy, sixty-year-old, Afro-American woman who greets everyone entering this world. She has the presence of a drill sergeant in a business suit, sporting a 50s-style hairdo. She stands almost six feet tall. I feel dwarfed around her. She is large and formidable with a gruff exterior but a heart as big as the city itself. Luella's job is to keep the waiting room running smoothly, assist those too injured or sick to register themselves, and monitor the number of visitors who go back to the treatment rooms. She is the first employee the patients encounter after walking through the main entrance to the emergency department. Her roles are varied. Sometimes she acts like a cop and at other times a public relations representative for the hospital. She observes those waiting to be treated and lets the triage nurse know if someone needs to be seen immediately.

I arrive at least ten minutes early so I am calm and grounded when I walk through the doors. I make a quick pit stop to my office, slide my identification card through the time card slot and head straight to the ER treatment areas. Unless a crisis situation is waiting for me, I always stop in each room to visit with all the new patients. A major part of my job is to get the patients to open up and share their deepest and most frightening thoughts at their most vulnerable times. After all, what is more profound than contemplating our own frailty or mortality?

I only spend a few minutes with a patient unless they need me to help solve a problem, so I have to work fast. I try to disarm with a smile, a touch, and a look to let them know that I care. I usually introduce myself, then I ask why they are in the hospital and if they are warm enough. I love passing out the heated blankets we keep in a large oven in a store room. In the first minute or two I pick up some intimate detail and use that information to create a bond between us. It is quite exhilarating when that moment occurs. Most of us are not used to verbal intimacy with a stranger. It seems especially uncomfortable for seniors. But when dealing with a crisis, whether their own or that of a loved one, their guard is down and many become uncharacteristically open and vulnerable. The smallest "perceived slights" can take on monumental importance. The wrong look or word, having no visitors, no telephone calls, not getting a glass of water, a blanket or immediate attention from the nursing staff can bring out intense feelings of loneliness and desperation. I am there to offer positive interaction. A smile and kind words can offer hope and inspiration as much as the best medical care available. I have witnessed the power to heal through this connection and have attempted to alleviate suffering through offering emotional catharsis. I am definitely NOT a neutral third party.

3

HEART ATTACK

"I THOUGHT IT WAS ONLY INDIGESTION"

It was September 9, 2001. After being paged, I walked into room eight. There was barely enough space for the four nurses, a respiratory therapist, and an emergency room doctor. They were all frantically working on a woman who had suffered a heart attack. Despite the urgency, someone spotted me standing in the back of the room and asked me to meet with the patient's friend who had accompanied the ambulance to the hospital.

I rushed out to the waiting room and found a devastated forty-something year-old woman with a slight frame. She was sobbing and her head was buried between her hands. She abruptly glanced up and noticed me standing in front of her. She leaped out of her seat and with a quivering voice she asked, "How is Mona? Is she going to make it? I can't lose her. I just can't lose her." She was frantic. I tried to calm her by introducing myself and asking her questions. She tearfully told me that her name was Sue and the patient's name was Mona. I suggested we sit down and she could fill me in on all the details of what had happened to her friend.

Mona, Sue, Myra, Julie, and Michele had decided to converge in Las Vegas to celebrate Michele's engagement. They traveled on different planes from their homes in Philadelphia, Chicago, Cleveland and New York City. As children, Mona and Sue had been next-door neighbors and the best of friends. They even attended the same college together. Mona and Sue spoke on the telephone at least once a month and never went longer than two years without visiting each other. The other women were good friends from high school. They had spent six months planning this trip and they were all thrilled to finally be here. They registered for two honeymoon suites at the Hard Rock Hotel and Casino.

The Hard Rock Hotel was chosen for its exciting atmosphere. This is the best place in town to spot young movie and television stars, top athletes, and famous musicians.

The casino is filled with rock and roll memorabilia, autographed photos, instruments, sheet music and anything else associated with the history of rock music. All of the staff are gorgeous and the clientele is just as entertaining. The women were ready to let their hair down and have fun on this vacation.

The next morning Mona woke up ahead of the others and decided to go for a walk. She returned an hour later complaining of chest pains. Sue suggested that Mona lie down for a short rest and Mona agreed. Within a half-hour, Mona announced that the pains had disappeared so they rounded up the others and agreed to go to the buffet for a late breakfast. All of the women indulged in tasty delights and ate and drank entirely too much.

After their meal, they decided to stroll through the casino and the gift shop. Suddenly, Mona's chest pains returned. She sat down at a blackjack table and took out an antacid from her purse. Sue admitted to me that she looked into Mona's purse and noticed that it was filled with over-the-counter, stomach-soothing medications of all brands. Mona tried to assure everyone that she would be fine if she just rested for a few minutes.

"It's nothing. Just a little indigestion." Mona declared. "Don't worry about me" The matter was quickly dropped. They accepted her proclamation of health and continued on with their sight-seeing tour.

Ten minutes passed when Mona frantically grabbed Sue's arm, pulled her away from the group, and pleaded with her, "Something's very wrong with me, Sue. I need to go to the hospital right away." Sue could see that Mona was sweating profusely and in a state of total panic. Sue ran up to a security guard in the casino and yelled "Call an ambulance right now! I think my friend is having a heart attack."

Mona was immediately escorted to the security office to lie down and was told to wait for medical assistance. Mona insisted that the others continue on with their day. "I'll be fine. Don't worry about me." Sue said she would call them later. Mona was not comfortable having all of this attention and did not want the other women to see her in pain.

The paramedics showed up within a few minutes. They immediately covered Mona's face with a mask and began administering oxygen. Mona's blood pressure and pulse rate were checked, rechecked, and recorded.

Moments later, Mona said that she was feeling better and did not need to go to a hospital. Because of Sue's insistence, Mona finally relented and the team transported the two of them to Sunrise Hospital.

When Mona arrived, she was immediately taken to a room in Station One. While changing into her hospital gown, she let out a shrill scream, clutched her chest, and began to gasp for air. She turned blue and stopped breathing. The staff rushed in just as Mona "coded." It took many heroic measures by the hospital staff to bring Mona back from the brink death. It was at that point that I personally became involved with Mona's case.

I assured Sue that I would check on Mona's condition and keep her informed every fifteen minutes. I left Sue in the waiting room and hurried backed to room eight for an update. Intravenous lines had been inserted into Mona's veins and numerous medications were being pumped into her body. The senior nurse was performing CPR by pushing down on Mona's upper chest. With each compression she called out: "One-Two-Three-Four-Five-rest. One-Two-Three-Four-Five-rest." Bev, the nurse, continued on as she dripped with perspiration and her arms strained from the exertion.

Then the doctor brought out two black paddles to administer electric shocks to Mona's chest. He placed them over her heart. The doctor called, "ALL CLEAR" to make sure that no one would be accidentally shocked by touching any metal part of the gurney. Then he pressed the button. The patient's body jolted and her back arched at least six inches off of the table. There were more manual pushes and the monitor indicated that a heartbeat had resumed.

Mona's heart stopped beating three times and three times the medical team would restart it. We were all holding our breath. "Keep trying!" the lead nurse shouted. "She is a forty year-old mother with two young children." The horror of the situation filled the room. The momentum accelerated and silent prayers raced through all of our minds. Just then, I spotted one of our best cardiologists walking through the emergency department to check up on another patient. One of the nurses immediately escorted him to room eight. No-one thought the patient would survive the next few minutes.

Thirty minutes passed before Mona was stabilized enough to be rushed to the Cath Lab so the cardiologist could assess the damage done to her heart. Once he had a full picture, he would then plan the next course of treatment - if only Mona could survive that long. Modern technology, medical knowledge, and more miracles were needed.

I returned to Sue in the waiting room and told her to follow me to the surgery waiting area. Though now in a different department, I decided to stay with Sue to provide comfort and support. I also agreed to be her eyes and ears during the catheterization process. I asked Sue more questions about Mona. She needed to talk and I was happy to listen. She said that Mona had been overweight all of her life. Mona was always very active and became totally immersed in whatever project she took on. Sue described her friend as a "definite type-A personality"; a real go-getter who burned the candle at both ends." Mona smoked a pack of cigarettes a day, a habit that began at age fourteen. She admired Mona's striving to be a wonderful wife and loving mother. Along with her responsibilities at home, Mona had recently been promoted to vice president of a mid-size computer software firm. Sue just couldn't believe that this was happening to her best friend. Mona always appeared to be in perfect health.

I assisted her with placing telephone calls to their worried friends at the hotel and to Mona's husband at home in Philadelphia. Sue's small frame continued to shake and her eyes were red-rimmed and swollen almost shut. Sue couldn't stop trying and she kept shaking her head in disbelief. "This just can't be happening." she repeated over and over. Since I couldn't predict the outcome, I just sat quietly and listened.

I left Sue to head back to the Cath Lab to check on Mona's progress. I found the procedure fascinating. I had never witnessed any type of surgery before and I peered out through the observation window in awe. The surgeon insert- ed what looked like a fishhook on a wire into one of the arter- ies bringing blood to the heart muscle. A lab technician was monitoring every movement on four computer screens in the tiny cubicle behind the window in the next room. Graphs and charts appeared on two of the monitors, and the other two screens were used to guide the doctor and nurses. It took only eight minutes to insert a tiny balloon into the collapsed artery on the left side of her heart. The balloon then pushed the plaque (buildup) to either side in order to open up the artery so that a stent could be inserted. A stent holds the artery open. This is vital to getting oxygenated blood to the heart. Suddenly the computer screen lit up with squiggly, throbbing movements of lines that indicated that the artery had been reopened and blood began pulsating throughout Mona's heart in a wide circular motion. It was a sight to see. I was suddenly aware of my own heart beating, and there was a new consciousness of my own life force. Mona had made it this far, but she was still in very critical condition.

When I returned to the surgery waiting room, I found Sue pacing restlessly. We made eye contact and she rushed over to me. "The operation is ove". I told her. "She made it through the procedure. Now we will have to wait and see how she responds, if the stent holds, and what her mental state is when she wakes up." I didn't want to tell Sue that there was a very real possibility of brain damage and that Mona may never again regain consciousness. This can happen when not enough blood goes to the brain during the time the person's heart is not beating. "Her recovery is now in the control of a much higher power." I said.

Sue began to cry again. She understood the seriousness of the situation, but she was also optimistic. "I have never been so frightened in my life." Sue told me. "This experience will change me forever. I will miss her so much if she dies." I did my best to reassure her without offering false hope. I told her that the next thirty-six hours would be critical for Mona's recovery.

I then escorted Sue to the waiting room of the intensive care unit to wait for Mona's husband to arrive from the airport. She was shivering so I wrapped her up in a warm blanket fresh out of the oven. Sue did not want to see Mona lying in a hospital bed, on a ventilator, and hooked up with wires to machinery. I continued to emphasize Sue's role in saving Mona's life. "If you hadn't insisted that Mona come to the hospital, she would be dead." I assured Sue. "Your friendship and love made the difference. Had she been at home, at work, or even with someone she was less comfortable with, she would have probably minimized the pain and put off getting treatment. How lucky she is to have you as a friend." Sue actually smiled. We hugged. I gave her my card and told her to call me anytime. When I left Sue, I returned to the emergency room. I was drained of emotion and I still had two hours left of my twelve-hour shift.

The next day, September 10, 2001, I clocked in and went directly to my office to check on Mona's status. I don't usually follow up with patients once they leave the emergency department as I interact with more than one hundred people everyday and I just don't have the time. But once my heart is totally engaged, I have to know how they are doing. I rushed to my office, turned on the computer and swiftly typed in Mona's name. I held my breath until her name appeared on the monitor. If a patient is deceased, a small "x" appears next to their name. I let out a long sigh of relief. There was no "x" next to Mona's name. She had made it through the night.

At my first opportunity, I hurried to the intensive care unit on the second floor. I desperately wanted to meet her. I had not yet seen Mona's face or spoken to her, but I felt as though I had known her for years. I slowly entered the room and saw her sleeping. She was attached to many machines that were making a lot of noise. All of the clicking and grinding indicated that Mona was still alive. I reached down and touched her left leg and foot. She was warm. I said a silent prayer and headed down the hall to the nurse's station to ask about Mona's progress. I was told that she had woken up early in the morning, but the nurse had sedated her again to allow her body to heal. Mona's hands were restrained by soft, cloth wrist bands, to prevent her from injuring her esophagus if she were to pull out the breathing tube of the ventilator.

The "vent" is a machine with a breathing tube connected to it that is inserted down the throat to assist the lungs in receiving the proper amounts of oxygen. This is done when a person is unable to breath sufficiently on their own. It is unnatural to have something stuck in our throats so the patient becomes agitated when consciously aware of it. Secretions are sucked out of the breathing passages by a small tube at regular intervals but the sensation is one of suffocation. I am told that it feels like being at the bottom of a swimming pool and not believing that you will be able to reach the surface in time. The experience can trigger a panic reaction if not sedated.

It was now September 11, 2001. I woke up to the news of the bombing of the World Trade Center and the Pentagon. Like so many Americans, I was overcome with sadness and outrage. My chest felt heavy during the entire drive to work. I knew that today would be intense. I arrived at work in a state of shock and disbelief.

Before clocking in, I went directly to ICU. I wanted to see how Mona was recovering. I desperately needed some good news today. I stood by Mona's bedside and just stared at her. I was deep in thought about the crisis in Mona's life and the events that had occurred in New York City and Washington just a few hours ago. Suddenly a nurse approached me. "Can I help you?" She inquired, "Are you a family member?" I told the nurse who I was and she informed me that there had been some difficult moments throughout the night, but Mona was doing much better now. The ventilator had even been removed; she was breathing on her own.

"How is her mental state?" I asked. Before she could answer, I blurted out, "What is the point of saving her life if she is now a vegetable?" I was appalled that I had just said that, but with all that had transpired today, I was not in a positive frame of mind.

Fortunately, the nurse didn't react to my bluntness. "Well," she said with a wide grin, "After Mona's husband had been here for an hour, she snapped at him to leave her alone so she could get some sleep. She must be doing okay." I had to laugh. Sue shared so many stories about Mona that this a comment I would have expected her to make. For the first time since she had arrived at the hospital, I was confident that Mona would be fine.

At that very moment, Mona rolled over in bed. The nurse looked at me, "I think she's awake. Would you like to speak to her?"

I can't even begin to describe how I felt. Goose pimples broke out all over my body and I shivered. My heart was filled with so much joy and relief. She had been a very strong presence in my life these past few days, yet we had never spoken. I had a goofy grin on my face when I approached her. I treasure that moment, for it gave my own life new meaning in the midst of such horrific events taking place elsewhere. We made eye contact for the first time and I had to fight back the tears.

"Mona, we have not met before, but I am so happy to see that you're awake and I can finally speak with you." I continued, "I'm the social worker from the emergency department and I spent many hours with Sue the night you were brought in. I've prayed for you ever since. I'm just thrilled that you are still with us and doing so well. You have a friend who loves you with all of her heart. Sue was so worried about you." "Was she really?" Mona asked. "Yes, and she shared many wonderful stories about your times together. I feel like I've known you for years, too." Mona seemed somewhat embarrassed by this statement. "You scared the hell out of all of us! Your friend saved your life by getting you here when she did."

Mona was speechless by what I had just said and her eyes filled up with tears. It was then that I noticed Mona's eyes; They were the clearest light blue I had ever seen. She was barely five feet tall and looked like a little girl in that large hospital bed. Her hair was deep red with frosted highlights and she had a stocky build. I breathed a deep sigh and let the good feelings surface.

Mona questioned me about the night she was brought in to the emergency room. Her memories ended at the time she had been placed into the ambulance. She was now alert and seemed very intelligent. I immediately liked her spirit. After speaking, she began to cough and spat up a little blood and phlegm. Mona was having a moderate amount of pain but was doing her best to maintain a brave facade. The nurse handed her a basin and then told her to lie back down to prevent any additional strain on her heart. She needed to rest. I wished her a speedy recovery and walked out of her room.

WOW! I felt like a huge weight had been lifted off of my shoulders. I had just witnessed another miracle, and I was even a small part of it. Knowing that Mona was doing well elevated my mood and gave me hope for the future.

Thousands of people died on this day and millions throughout the country would be grieving for them. The world was in a state of red alert; The possibility of another world war lurked. We were all stunned, yet, in my small part of the planet, this moment was incredible. Mona had been given a second chance at life.

I felt infinity better than when I first arrived at work today. I returned to the emergency department with a smile on my face, ready for my next challenge.

I stopped by the waiting room on my way back to the ER. I wanted to assess the mood of the patients. It was crowded as usual but the atmosphere was very different today. Fifty people were sitting there but the room was noise-free. No-one was talking. They were all glued to the three television sets broadcasting different scenes from New York City. The pain and suffering around us seemed dwarfed by the magnitude of the disasters.

MR. CADILLAC

The weather had finally changed and winter settled in. This day the high temperature was 58 degrees. Although cold and windy, it was a typical sunny day in "Sin City." An ambulance roared up to the entrance of the hospital, lights flashing, sirens blasting. I was outside at the time and watched the paramedics unload a man barely clinging to life. He was Caucasian and appeared to be in his 60's. He had a barrel chest that seemed much too big to hold up his otherwise medium frame and a long, wide scar ran down his sternum, an obvious sign of previous heart surgery. His belly was swollen and he was balding in the usual places. His eyes were slightly opened but appeared to be glazed and unfocused.

The man had three gold chains around his neck, a diamond earring in his left earlobe, and two gold bracelets on his left wrist. He wore cowboy boots and blue jeans, but no shirt. His appearance struck me as someone desperately attempting to recapture his youth, but he was seriously out of step with the times. No one knew his name so I grabbed the paramedic's report to see where he had been picked up and found a contact name and phone number. I searched the patient's wallet for more clues and found an "emergency contact" list with two numbers on it. One was "Brian" with a Denver telephone number and the other one was "Kathy" with a Northern California telephone number.

I dialed the contact number from the report and was instantly connected to a mechanic at a local Cadillac dealership. He told me that the patient's name was Harry and he was a regular customer. The mechanic had just informed Harry that the repairs on his leased 2000 vehicle would run $6,000. They were discussing whether Harry should lease a new car or pay to have the current one repaired. Mid-sentence, Harry grabbed his chest and collapsed. He then passed out and fell to the floor. The mechanic yelled out for someone to call 911 and he began performing CPR on Harry until the paramedics arrived. He was traumatized by the event, but I assured him that his actions helped Harry survive up to this point. I said that I personally believed that Good Samaritans show up when needed and he should feel very proud of what he had done today. His voice cracked and he began to cry. "You were a hero today. Feel good about that." I said before hanging up.

After an update from the doctor on Harry's condition, I decided to place the difficult call to Brian in Denver. There are no right words to tell someone that a loved one is in critical condition and may not survive. Brian answered the phone and I asked if he knew Harry. He told me that Harry was his father, so I enlightened him about the seriousness of his Dad's condition. For a moment there was only silence. Brian was stunned and when he did speak, his voice collapsed with emotion. He promised to take the next plane out and would get to Las Vegas as quickly as possible. I told Brian that I would be at work until midnight and to ask for me as soon as he arrived at the hospital. I asked if he knew who Kathy was and he informed me that she was his sister and she was living in San Francisco. He wanted to be the one to make the call. I was relieved that I did not have to do it.

I hustled myself back to Harry's bedside. Harry was put on a ventilator to assist with his breathing but he struggled anyway. He kept having seizures, his feet and hands jerked continuously and his pupils were fixed and dilated. The situation did not look good. I kept looking at my watch and hoping that Brian would arrive in time to say his good-byes to his Dad.

I checked on Harry every fifteen minutes. I touched his forehead and whispered in his ear. "Hang in there, Harry. You're going to be fine. Brian and Kathy are on their way here to be with you. They both love you very much." I repeated this to him many times, hoping that he might hear me and fight harder for his life.

Three hours later, I was paged and told that I was needed in room seven. Sitting in a chair, leaning over Harry, was a very handsome, thirty-two-year old man with jet black hair and large, sad green eyes. He was distraught and tears were streaming down both sides of his face. I introduced myself but when he tried to speak, his voice again filled with emotion. "This man made me everything I am today, both good and bad. How can I ever repay him? What can I do to make him better?"

Obviously this was Harry's son, Brian and I thought my heart would break watching him. He needed to vent and to have me just "be there" and listen. There were no magic words that would make the situation less painful for him.

I left for a few minutes to take care of some unfinished business so I could give Brian my full attention. I knew that the night was going to be a long one for him. When I returned, he picked up where he had left off. Brian said, "Dad and Mom are getting a divorce after forty-four years of marriage and Kathy and I both stopped speaking to him after he walked out on Mom two years ago. "He just has to pull through; I have so much to make up to him." Brian regretted taking sides, but after witnessing my own parents divorce after thirty-five years, I understood how that could happen. I tried to help him let go of his guilt.

I looked up and suddenly noticed that a Filipino woman had standing in the doorway. She was petite and appeared to be in her late thirties, her hair was very dark brown and she was wearing sunglasses in an attempt to hide her grief. I surmised that she was either the "other woman" or another important person in Harry's life. I watched Brian's mood change. She tried to muster a faint smile but quickly dropped her head after seeing the hate that raged in Brian's eyes.

Two minutes passed when another man showed up at the edge of the room. He briskly walked past "her" and went directly to Brian. They embraced for a moment. He was quite handsome, tall and slender with beautiful, thick, blond hair. I could tell by their interaction that he and Brian were lovers. He signaled Brian to leave the room with him so they could talk outside. I heard him tell Brian to be nice to her, that his father must love her, that she was obviously in pain and hurting too. Brian agreed and approached the Filipino woman when he re-entered the room. They were conversing quietly when she let it slip out that she and Harry had been in love for the last ten years. I find it fascinating to watch people, in times of stress, trip over their own guilt, and say things they were attempting to hide. Or maybe, subconsciously, she wanted Brian to know how important she was to Harry.

After this revelation, a visibly shaken Brian returned to his father's bedside. He held Harry's hand and kept repeating the things he wanted to say to his father, but found too difficult to reveal when his dad was conscious. He found it easier to speak to Harry now that his dad was in a coma. The emotions just kept pouring out of Brian.

The "other woman" sat quietly beside Harry on the other side of the bed but never again interacted with Brian. She was very uncomfortable, she wiggled in her chair and held her head between trembling hands. She was enduring the pain in her own way, privately.

A short time later Harry was taken to the Cath Lab where the medical team attempted to repair his heart. Afterwards, he was transferred to the intensive cardiac care unit; His condition remained extremely critical.

The next day, I checked my computer as soon as I arrived at work. I had thought about Harry, Brian, Brian's lover and the "other woman" for much of the evening. I just had to know how he was progressing. He was still listed with no "x" beside his name so I knew that Harry had survived the procedure and made it through the night.

I left the emergency room and walked up to the third floor to check in on him. The "other woman" was not there. I found Brian and his partner sitting beside Harry's bed. Brian was furious. He became loud and animated as he told me what had transpired after I left the room last evening. "She" told Brian that Harry had written a new will and that neither Brian nor his sister had any control in any matters pertaining to Harry. "Very bad timing on her part." I thought. First thing that morning, Brian left the hospital to hire both an attorney and a private investigator to determine his father's assets and to secure Harry's estate. Brian was also taking legal action to have the court declare him as the trustee and executor. Brian seemed much more composed and more accepting of his father's pending death now. His rage kept his mind off of the tragedy right in front of him.

Harry's tests showed that he was brain dead and body death was imminent and would happen soon. Kathy, Brian's sister, was engaged to be married. The ceremony was planned for the following month in San Francisco. Kathy convinced her fiancee to meet her in Las Vegas and move up the wedding date. She had always wanted to have her father at her wedding so she decided to hire a minister, decorate the hospital room with flowers, and dress Harry in a tuxedo so she could fulfill her dream. I understood her situation but couldn't believe that she would want the memory of her wedding day associated with her father lying in a hospital bed, in a coma, near death. I was informed that they planned to disconnect the breathing machine right after the ceremony. I had no desire to attend. Harry left quite a mess to be sorted out by all who loved him.

"I didn't want to complain"

Late one night, a sixty-seven year old man arrived in the ER via helicopter transport from Bullhead, Arizona, a small town about one hundred miles outside of Las Vegas. His heart had stopped twice and he had been shocked back to life. I was asked to meet with his wife and explain the situation to her. The prognosis was grim and I was told to prepare her for the worst. One of his cardiologists described his condition as a "train wreck" and he was not expected to survive beyond the next few hours.

His wife was a pleasant, small-town woman, about the same age as her husband. Mary spoke with a Southern accent and was wearing a gray sweatshirt and black polyester pants covered with dirt. She apologized for her appearance but said she had been working in the yard when her husband had his attack. She was calm but it was obvious that she needed to talk to someone. I escorted her to the "Quiet Room" and told her that I would be happy to sit with her while the doctor did his job.

During the next two hours I got to know her quite well. She and Roy had met in junior high school, dated all through high school, and married at age eighteen. Neither of them had any other serious relationships. He had, single-handedly, built up an electrical and air conditioning installation and repair business and, according to Mary, he had done extremely well. They had three children, now grown, and four grandchildren.

Ironically, she had been the one with many medical crises throughout the years. Her husband was the caretaker in their relationship and she was comfortable with their respective roles.

Two weeks before this attack, he began complaining of neck and back pains and was tired all of the time. His heartburn had also become a major problem. He was a diabetic, too. He had not acted very concerned about his physical health. However, he had initiated many conversations with Mary and his family about updating his will. He even discussed funeral arrangements and what he thought Mary should do after his death. I call these talks "Callings from God." Don't ignore them!

Many of our patients report a strong sense of pending doom prior to a major medical emergency. Some disregard these signals until it is too late. Roy, like many of us, had little knowledge of the symptoms of a heart attack. He had ignored weeks of warnings and chose to take over-the-counter medications and antacids instead of seeking medical attention.

Mary told me that she, along with friends and family members, had tried to cajole Roy into seeing a doctor. He remained stubborn right up to the moment he keeled over in his own living room. I had the sinking feeling that Roy would not make it.

The odds seemed to be stacked against him.

An hour passed and Mary was getting restless. We were both anxious to know what was happening. Based on his test results, the cardiologists were not optimistic about his chances for survival. I asked his nurse if I could bring the patient's wife back to see Roy. The nurse would allow her to stay for only five minutes because there was much work to be done and time was of the essence.

I returned to the Quiet Room to give Mary the news. I warned her that Roy had been intubated and explained that he was in extremely critical condition. I wanted to begin preparing her for what seemed to be an inevitable outcome.

Mary approached Roy's bed cautiously with fear and trepidation. She stood at least ten feet from the gurney where he was hooked up with wires and tubes connected to various machines. He had three different plastic bags filled with various intravenous drugs and a large ventilator tube protruding from his mouth. The equipment was beeping away with alarms and red lights constantly reminding us that something was very wrong.

I gently put my hand on Mary's shoulder. "Touch him. It's okay." I assured her. "You should talk to him and let him know what happened and where he is now. He may be able to hear you and you need to reassure him."

She immediately began rubbing his head and caressing his hair. She leaned over, kissed his forehead, and whispered in his ear all the events of the past few hours. She did not cry, although I could tell that it was taking tremendous effort to suppress her tears.

I said, "Roy has many strikes against him and, at this point, only God knows if he will make it or not." She reached for his hand and gave it a soft squeeze.

When we returned to the Quiet Room, her sister-in-law and husband had arrived. Stella wanted to see her brother but was afraid to go in alone. Her husband did not want to accompany her, but I assured Stella that I would stay with her the entire time. Walking to Roy's room, Stella proceeded to blame Mary for Roy's condition. "Mary is always ill with one thing or another and nags Roy all the time." Stella bitterly complained. That's why he had this heart attack. It's because of her!"

At this point, I did not confront her or dispute what she was saying. I believed that the major problems were Roy's cavalier attitude towards his health and his choice to ignore all the signs that were telling him that something was very wrong. Holding back her tears, Stella saw Roy briefly, and then slowly walked back to the Quiet Room to wait with Mary.

Two of the three cardiologists on Roy's case came into the Quiet Room and spoke briefly with the family. They were honest with their opinions and did not give them much hope. They admitted Roy's chances were bleak, at best. The doctors would be taking Roy to the Cath Lab to check for blockages and damage to the heart. There was also concern about Roy's brain function. No one knew how long his brain had been deprived of oxygen. The doctors made it clear that Roy might not survive the procedure. They added that there was also a possibility that even if he did survive, he might never regain consciousness. The mood in the room was almost suffocating with plenty of guilt and blame to go around. Family members often feel responsible for not insisting that their loved-one see a doctor.

I escorted the family to the surgery waiting room. We all hugged and I told them to think positive thoughts. I assured them that anything could happen and that I had witnessed many miracles. I had to leave then and walked down the long hallway to wait for the next crisis to hit.

I was off work for the next three days but could not get Roy out of my mind. I frequently thought about him and his wife and wondered how they were doing. I felt a strong bond with Mary and Stella so I decided to call in to find out Roy's status. Caroline was on duty so she brought his chart up on the computer for me. I held my breath while I heard her tapping on the keyboard, trying to prepare myself for the worst. I had very little faith that he would survive. I kept remembering the cardiologist referring to Roy's heart as a "total disaster." Roy had simply waited too long to seek treatment. Then Caroline shared great news! He was still alive, although very critical. This was very encouraging.

As soon as I returned to work, I ran to my computer to check on Roy for myself. I typed in his name and my heart began to race as the cursor began to blink. There was no little "x" beside his name so I decided to head upstairs to his room to see for myself how he was progressing.

I expected to find Mary sitting next to the bed. But I found Roy still unconscious and only his nurse was with him. My heart sank. Where was Mary? Did she collapse under the stress of being the caretaker? The nurse asked if I was a family member. When I explained who I was, the nurse said he was doing fair and had a fifty-fifty chance of pulling through. She added that Mary had been there constantly and that she had finally gone home to get some much-needed sleep. Their children had arrived from Southern California and Oklahoma and they had also been keeping a constant vigil. I walked away feeling sad and discouraged since fifty-fifty odds weren't that great and I thought that Roy should have either been awake or dead by this point.

The next day, I again checked on Roy in the computer. Still ok. Then I scanned through the nurses' notes and the most recent entry filled my heart with warmth. "Patient awake and alert; Well oriented to time, date and place; Sitting up in bed. Patient reports feeling tired and weak but is eating and drinking."

I rushed out of my office and stopped at Station One to inform the charge nurse that I was heading upstairs for one of my "Remarkable Trips." My co-workers know what that means as my excitement radiates throughout the emergency room every time it happens. "I am off to see a miracle!" I loudly proclaimed. "I will be back in fifteen minutes." I hurried as fast as I could, my heart was beating faster and faster as I wove my way throughout the hospital corridors to the elevator. I was very excited about meeting Roy. I had waited five days for this and didn't want to waste another minute.

He was unconscious when he first arrived. Prior to today, Roy was a rather large, balding, older gentleman, who laid in a coma in room number eight. I had no idea what his voice sounded like or how he smiled. Even the color of his eyes were a mystery to me.

I entered his room to find a nice looking man about my father's age, sitting up in a chair. Our eyes met. Mine began to fill with tears. His eyes were pastel blue and he looked kind, and gentle, and very tired. He cocked his head abruptly when I entered the room. My first words to him were, "Hi miracle man. Boy, am I happy to finally meet you." My voice filled with elation. "You had us all really worried."

Mary was there and she introduced us. I told him how very close he came to death and how much we had all prayed for him. "I guess it just wasn't your time, yet. I think you are still meant to do something special in this life; Your work here just isn't done yet." I could feel my soul begin to soar. At times like these, I can hardly handle the blissful feelings rushing through my body.

Within minutes, Mary began to nag at him. "Hurry up and get well, Roy. I need you back home to take care of me." I looked at his face and thought, "I wonder if he is happy to still be here?" I looked at her and calmly said, "Don't get on his case just yet. He just woke up." I turned to Roy and said, "You need to focus on yourself and on getting your strength back. That's what's important right now." To my amazement, Roy smiled at me and said, "You are right. Mary, damn it—quit nagging me." I sensed that this may have been the first time in fifty years that he had stood up to his wife.

Mary jumped out of her seat to hug me. She was grateful that I was with her through out the worst part of her nightmare. I hugged her back, patted Roy on his arm and left the room to return to the ER to share the wonderful news with my co-workers.

I literally bumped into the nurse who had taken care of Roy on the first night that he was in the emergency room. "Hey Joe, remember the "code" Roy from the other night? He was in room eight. "Yeh." he answered. "What's up?" "You saved his life, Joe. He is going to make it. I just spoke to him and he looks good." The nurse's face lit up like a small child on Christmas morning. Smiling broadly, he questioned me on all of the details. He beamed from ear to ear as I relayed what I knew. I could tell that all his years of education, experience, and financial sacrifices were suddenly validated. At this moment, he had no doubt that he had made the right career choice.

I am driven to follow up on critical cases whenever I spend a lot of time with the families. Maybe I feel it so intensely because I am still a novice at dealing with crises and death, but I hope it never becomes "just another day at work." I come away from "miracles" being thrilled to be alive and happy to be a part of the process. It is an emotional prime rib and lobster dinner for me. This part of my work is totally satisfying.

HYPOCHRONDRIASIS

"Are heart Attacks Contagious?"

I always believed that heart attacks only happen to those over the age of fifty. This is definitely a misnomer. Many patients under forty come into the ER with chest pains and palpitations. Sometimes it turns out to be panic attacks triggered by extreme stress and other times there are significant heart problems.

I began to experience my own mortality at the age of fifty-two and turned to a cardiologist for reassurance. The heart is the one organ we can actually feel working and, through thought or action, we can often temporarily slow it down or speed up the beat. Because of this awareness, once malfunction is suspected, it is extremely difficult to ignore.

Like many people, I worried about a possible heart attack,

the parking lot and after spending ten minutes contemplating what to do, I decided to go into the emergency room. I signed in and was immediately taken to triage where the nurse got my insurance information and took my blood pressure and temperature. She then escorted me back to the chest pain section where I undressed and climbed into a flimsy gown that offered no modesty. It's amazing what you think about when you are on the other side of emergency room care. Why do the gowns have to be so drab? Why do they have to tie at the neck but open in the back? Although I had been admitted to hospitals before for minor surgeries, this was a totally new experience and gave me an entirely different perspective. The room décor, the sounds, even the room temperature became very important.

The nurse attended to me almost immediately. I told him where I worked and added that I was too self-conscious to go there. I wanted him to know that I was a comrade, hoping that this would get me better care. After a few moments of chit-chat, he placed two small hoses in my nostrils and turned on the oxygen machine. I flinched at first, expecting an offensive odor. There was none. Then an EKG technician placed little round electrodes with adhesives on various parts of my chest and connected me up to the EKG machine. Immediately a tape began spitting out zigzag lines which measured the electricity generated by my beating heart. A blood pressure monitoring device was inflated around my right bicep. The numbers changed every few minutes. The nurse then sprayed a few shots of nitroglycerin in my mouth. He told me that I might get a bad headache from it, but that it would be a normal reaction. He waited with me for a few minutes to monitor how my body would handle it. I did get a headache but not as bad as expected. My blood pressure, which was high at first, came down to within the normal range.

Next, a portable chest x-ray machine was brought to my bedside. X-rays were taken and blood was drawn to test for any abnormalities. For the next two hours nothing happened. I laid on this very uncomfortable bed, obsessing over whether it would be better to have something wrong or to feel foolish for seeking help. I heard the sounds of the intercom, knowing what the codes meant. I listened in on staff conversations and to the moans and groans of other patients. I could tell how serious a situation was just from the sounds. At one point, I heard a female patient scream to be left alone. Her protests continued for about five minutes. I thought I recognized the voice and asked my nurse if it was Sherry Brown, a psychiatric patient that came to my hospital often. Sure enough, it was Sherry. She was making my headache worse. I was very annoyed, impatient and I longed for silence.

I was anxious for the results. Why does it have to take so darn long? What were they doing? After a few hours, I wanted out. I called my nurse and asked how much longer it would be. "Soon." he said. The patients at the hospital I work at usually wait up to two hours to get test results. I now understood their frequent requests and resulting bad temperaments. For the first time since beginning my job in the emergency room, I was able to fully understand what our patients went through.

Another hour passed before I saw the doctor. He said that everything came back fine but he wanted me to stay in the chest pain unit for twenty-four hours for observation. I declined the offer and signed out, promising to see my cardiologist at my scheduled appointment time. I left the hospital feeling very proud of myself for having the courage to do what I knew needed to be done. My palpitations and insomnia continued, but I was less apprehensive.

I was relieved when the day of my appointment finally arrived. The doctor's waiting room was crowded; fifty men and women filled every seat. I was the youngest one there that day. I waited two hours (the usual wait in Las Vegas where doctors are in short supply), and then was escorted to an examination room. Again, my blood pressure was taken and an echo ultrasound was done of my heart to measure heart muscle activity. Totally painless. My blood pressure was elevated and I was told that I had a heart murmur but everything else looked fine. He gave me a pocket - sized card to carry in my wallet and instructed me to take antibiotics prior to having any invasive dental work done to reduce the risk of infection. He also gave me a holter monitor to wear while I slept which would measure cardiac events that occurred during the night and the pounding that I felt upon awakening. The doctor prescribed Benicar for the high blood pressure and asked me to return in a few weeks.

While there were no significant medical problems with my heart, I was still not sleeping. I decided to get tested at a sleep clinic. I arrived at 9:00 p.m., got hooked up to a number of electrodes across my chest and went to sleep. I was diagnosed with restless leg syndrome, which means my legs move all night long. I was prescribed a light sedative and was gradually able to sleep longer each night.

I am glad that I went through all of the procedures and I will not hesitate to do so again if the problem returns. Anyone, male or female, young or old, can have heart problems. Early detection can mean the difference between living a full life and being incapacitated or dying earlier than necessary.

HEART ATTACK FACTS

Myocardial infarction, also referred to as a heart attack, is by far the most common cause of death in the emergency room. Many of our patients were unaware that a heart attack was happening to them. There were warning signs, but they were either ignored or rationalized and dismissed. They blamed the pains on indigestion or anxiety.

So much is reported about the need to keep our cholesterol levels in check. This is because a heart attack can be caused by the formation of a blood clot around cholesterol plaque. These plaques are located on the inner walls of the arteries leading to the heart. Cholesterol is a fatty chemical, which is part of the outer lining of cells in the body. It forms into a hard, thick substance, or plaque, within the artery wall and can cause a narrowing of the artery. This process begins during the late teenage years, due to the "junk food" diet of most American teenagers which contains large amounts of cholesterol. Smoking, high blood pressure and diabetes also accelerate the accumulation of plaque. This process is called atherosclerosis.

When we exercise or get excited, the narrowed coronary arteries can't increase the blood supply to meet the increased need of oxygen to the heart muscle. When the heart muscle is deprived of blood oxygen, ischemia results. This is often associated with a type of chest pain called angina. Typically, this occurs with exertion but subsides with rest. That is why so many of our patients feel better after a few hours of lying in a hospital bed. They are ready to go home and dismiss the entire episode as a fluke. I always smile and tell them that the decrease in pain is very normal but what happened earlier to bring them to us was not. When the narrowing in the artery becomes critical, the pain continues even if the patient is at rest.

Early heart attack deaths can sometimes be avoided if a bystander begins CPR (cardiopulmonary resuscitation) within the first five minutes of the ventricular fibrillation. Every one of us needs to be trained in this life-saving procedure and take annual refresher courses. CPR involves performing a procedure where the helper actually breathes for the victim. External chest compressions are applied to force the heart to pump. While one person performs CPR, have another call 911 immediately. The paramedics will attempt to stabilize the person's condition and get them to the hospital as quickly as possible. Paramedics can administer life-saving medications and even electric shock to force the heart to return to its normal beat before permanent damage occurs.

One million Americans suffer from a heart attack every year. Four hundred thousand will die as a result. Many heart attack deaths happen before the victim can reach any medical assistance. The good news is that with quick medical attention, a large majority of heart attack victims will survive if they get to a hospital in time.

I have witnessed hundreds of heart attacks and can attest to the urgency of seeking medical help right away. Other early warning signs include pain in the jaws; a shooting pain in the arms, usually the left arm; chest pain and indigestion. The latter is a very common red flag. Over and over again, I hear people blame spicy foods, a late night, and alcohol for the pains. Of course, heartburn may be just heartburn, but why take chances with your life. Even if it is acid-reflux, it still needs to be treated with medications. You still need to see a doctor and get it checked out if it continues beyond a short period of time. If it is heart disease or a pending heart attack, you will have a much greater chance of surviving if treated early.

HEART DISEASE IN WOMEN

Many myths surround women and cardiovascular disease. The first belief is that cardiovascular disease affects only middle-aged men. This is not true. Approximately one in four

American women have one or more forms of this disease. According to Karen Arcotta, MD, of the University of Nevada School of Medicine, the statistics show that more than fifty million women have high blood pressure. Another eleven million have coronary heart disease. One point three million women have rheumatic heart disease. Heart disease occurs in one in ten women between the ages of forty-five and sixty-four and in three out of ten women sixty-five or older.

The second myth is that hormone replacement therapy negates the risk of cardiovascular heart disease in post-menopausal women. The third is that the course of the disease is more benign in women.

The truth is that women have a higher number of major risk factors for cardiac disease than men. More than forty percent of all coronary events in women are fatal within one year. For men, only twenty-seven are fatal. The real shock is that sixty-six percent of all sudden deaths related to his disease occur in women with NO history of heart problems.

During routine office visits, women are less likely to be counseled about the importance of nutrition, exercise and weight reduction. The following statistics come from the Centers for Disease Control and the Prevention National Medical Care Survey who reviewed more than 29,000 routine office visits. One study found that only eight percent of the women questioned identified heart disease or stroke as their biggest health concern. In one year more women die from heart disease than from breast and cervical cancer combined. There are some major risk factors which can be controlled to improve these numbers. Twenty-three percent of women continue to smoke while one-fourth of all women have no regular sustained physical activity. Fifty-two percent of women forty-five years and older have high blood pressure while forty percent over fifty have high serum cholesterol. Factors you can't control include family history, age and menopause.

So, what can you do to reduce your odds of getting heart disease? Lose weight, increase physical activity, quit smoking, reduce stress, reduce alcohol consumption, eat a balanced diet and have your cholesterol levels checked often.

Cardiovascular disease is not an "event" but rather an ongoing progressive disease process. You need to discuss these issues with your doctor. Become knowledgeable about your blood pressure and cholesterol levels. Know where you stand. These are not just statistics; these are real women. I meet them every day in the emergency room.

4

Struggles After The Bombing

Our tourist patient count dropped dramatically the first few weeks following the attacks. We saw a large increase in complaints of chest pain, insomnia, shortness of breath, panic attacks and other stress-related problems with no identifiable physical origins.

The mentally-marginal were filling up our rooms with suicidal thoughts and actions and other generalized anxieties. One woman was convinced that she had met Osama Bin Laden after he dropped two bombs on Las Vegas Boulevard, right on top of the "Empire State Building" (a casino on the "strip" that is a replica of the one in New York).

The skies were noticeably quiet; The usual constant stream of aircraft noise was barely audible. Traffic on the "strip" was considerably lighter. For one month I couldn't write a single word as I was in a state of shock like everyone else.

The atmosphere in the hospital seemed eerie and disconcerting. Staff and patients alike were fixated on the constant blare of bad news emanating from numerous television sets through-out the treatment areas. We were all waiting for another disaster to strike. The staff acted much more subdued. Nothing seemed important anymore by comparison to what was happening on the east coast.

Persons of middle eastern descent were viewed with suspicion. One such patient arrived in a catatonic state. He could not speak, move, or even blink his eyes. My first reaction was one of fear. I suggested to the doctor that he should perform a body cavity search on the patient to be certain that he had not hidden any weapons inside one of his orifices. The doctor dismissed my concerns outright as being unnecessary.

ANTHRAX SCARE

The media became saturated with reports of an imminent biological or chemical attack. Our worse fears overtook our daily thoughts. The nation was obsessed. It took only thirty-one days for those fears to become reality.

The first case of anthrax poisoning was reported on October 12, 2001. Within days, anthrax and Cipro became household words. It didn't take long for the panic to hit Las Vegas. Ten days later I was called to Fast Track, (our urgent care section of the department for less serious cases). Jennifer, a thin, nervous, twenty-six year old woman, looked up when I entered her room. Jennifer's only complaint was that she had an infection in her right leg caused by a dog bite that happened five months earlier. The doctor ordered a blood test to determine the type of infection. An ultrasound test was performed on her leg as well. Both tests came back negative. There was absolutely nothing wrong with her leg. Instead of being relieved, she became loud and hostile. She did not care that her leg was fine. She wanted some medicine and that was that! The doctor could not get through to her so he left the room and called for me to intervene. My job was to speak with her and calm her down.

I showed her the test results and reiterated that she was fine. "If the leg continues to hurt, you should see a bone specialist for further tests." I explained. My words fell on deaf ears. "What's wrong with you people?" she screamed. "It's not as though I'm asking for morphine or any pain killers. I just want some antibiotics for my infected leg." She began to cry and shake. I tried to be compassionate with her. "We can't just give you medicine when there is nothing wrong. Besides, there are many different types of antibiotics and different ones treat different problems." She stormed out, clearly unhappy with us all.

The next day I was called into my supervisor's office. "We received a complaint against you." Ann said. "Do you remember the woman with the dog bite? She said that you refused to give her any antibiotics because you were hoarding them all for the anthrax cases." I couldn't believe what I was hearing. At first I was too surprised to say anything. I totally missed Jennifer's true purpose for coming in, which would explain why she had been so upset when we refused her request. It had never crossed my mind that she was panicked about being exposed to anthrax.

Since that day we have had a dozen patients who have wanted to be tested for anthrax and I have become much more sensitive to these issues. Lesson learned.

These scenarios added to my feelings of dread for what was happening in America. I worried about becoming contaminated by a patient and I no longer felt safe at work. Every hour I walked outside the emergency department looking for suspicious packages or people lurking around. I spent more time in the waiting room area so I could assess the mood of the group. I dwelled on whether the hospital was prepared for an attack and how would I handle it if disaster did hit home.

Our patient census went back up to normal within a few weeks and I realized that life does go on. We would all need to adjust to the craziness and heightened paranoia surrounding us and the effects of this would become a part of my daily routine at work.

5

DIABETES

"It's too much trouble to test myself"

Many people arrive at the emergency room suffering from serious complications of diseases that can be managed easily with medication and other preventative measures. Diabetes is one such disease.

It was Mother's Day and Dr. Green asked me to meet with Mrs. Rodriquez, a 49-year-old woman, suffering from generalized weakness, numbness in her left foot, and she was struggling with her mobility. She was diagnosed with diabetes a year before but had never bothered to fill her insulin prescription. Now Mrs. Rodriquez was in the emergency room, extremely ill and barely able to function. Denial can be deadly. Her doctors and nurses were exhausted from their attempts to get her to understand the seriousness of her condition. Their words had fallen on deaf ears.

I struggled with how to approach her about her disease. Did she fully understand the seriousness of the situation and what would happen to her if she didn't monitor and control her sugar levels? I needed to know what motivated her.

As I entered her room, I decided to take a heavy-handed approach. Every other approach had just not gotten through to her. Mrs. Rodriquez was lying in bed. She looked much older than forty-nine. She was pale and appeared weak and depressed. It was even difficult for her to sit up. The clothes beside the bed were attractive and expensive. She had a matching purse and shoes. Her jewelry included a beautiful amethyst ring on her right hand and a diamond wedding ring on her left hand. A young woman sitting beside her looked like a younger version of Mrs. Rodriquez. I walked in with a big smile and said "Happy Mother's Day. My name is Marsha and I am the social worker here in the emergency room. Is this your daughter?"

"Yes, this is Carmen." she said in a monotone voice. Her affect was completely flat. "Are you a mother, too?" I asked the younger woman. "Yes, I have a two year-old son." she replied.

"Happy Mother's Day to you, too." I paused for a moment. In a warm and concerned voice, I turned towards Carmen and continued, "I want to tell you a story of what may be waiting in the near future. Imagine that it's Mother's Day a few years from now. The weather is sunny, flowers are beginning to bloom and it is a great day to be alive. But Carmen, you wake up depressed and begin to cry. You know that you will spend a big part of the day at the cemetery visiting your mother's grave. Your mother died needlessly from complications of diabetes. She didn't take her medication, so she slipped into a diabetic coma and after three weeks, passed away." I glanced at Mrs. Rodriquez, then back again at Carmen who was shifting in her seat. "You blame yourself. 'How could this have happened?' you ask yourself over and over again. "What could I have done to prevent this? What could I have said to my mother to make her understand how serious this is if left untreated?" "Your heart is heavy. You're lonely and you long to confide in her as you always have done in the past. But it's too late. She's gone. She died prematurely from a disease that could have been easily controlled."

They both began to cry. I felt a little guilty about using emotional manipulation, but I also knew that the logical approach had been unsuccessful and her life may depend on my ability to get through to her and her daughter. "I don't have the money for the medicine." begged Mrs. Rodriquez. Carmen, shocked, just sat there wiping her eyes. I wondered if Mrs. Rodriquez had even told her daughter about the diabetes or if Mrs. Rodriquez fully understood it herself. People often hear what they want to hear, especially if it is bad news.

"You have no choice." I told Mrs. Rodriquez firmly. "You must make buying insulin your priority. I've noticed that your clothes are expensive and your nails look professionally manicured. Instead of these luxuries, you need to spend your money on your medication. It has to be a top priority. This is so important. Please believe me, I am not just trying to scare you."

Just then my pager sounded and I was needed elsewhere. I excused myself and said that I would be back as soon as possible.

Two hours later, I returned to speak with Mrs. Rodriquez again. This time she was alone. Carmen had left the hospital to spend part of the day with her own family.

I told Mrs. Rodriquez that all the lectures were over. I assured her that I was only here to help her and I asked her if she had thought about what I had said earlier. She nodded affirmatively. She seemed a little stronger now. Her blood sugar level was back in balance and she was feeling much better. "Carmen and her husband agreed to pay for my insulin until I can go back to work." Then she confided, "I am terrified of needles and don't know how to use them. No one showed me how. Could you?" "Ah-ha!" I thought. This might be one of the main reasons that she had not followed the doctor's orders.

I smiled and said, "I would be happy to get your nurse to teach you before you leave today. It will take a little while for you to get used to the procedure but it doesn't hurt and soon it will become second nature." I was thrilled that I had gotten through to her. What I call "tough love" worked again, this time even better than I had imagined.

After she was discharged, Dr. Green stopped me in the hall to ask what I had done to finally convince her to begin her insulin injections. I shared with him what I had said to the patient and her daughter. Dr. Green replied "Interesting approach. It must have worked because she insisted on getting a new prescription from me and she planned to go right to the pharmacy to fill it. Good work." I beamed and moved on to my next client.

Repeating Family Patterns

A month later, a young mother of a three-year old came in with the same symptoms as Mrs. Rodriquez. She was weak and had numbness in her feet. She felt unsteady and light headed. I spoke with her about her insulin intake. She told me she couldn't afford the medication or the testing equipment. From her appearance, I surmised that she had little income.

"I know all about diabetes." she quipped. "My mother died from diabetic complications when I was fourteen years old." I was shocked at her apathy. She knew first hand what it is like to grow up without a mother.

Her name was Shannon. She was married and her husband had recently quit his job to take an extended vacation.

According to Shannon, it did not matter to him that his family was being destroyed because of his laziness. Shannon told me she could not work because she felt so weak. She also said that she could not earn enough to cover baby-sitting costs. It was a big effort just to pay the rent. She was not interested in hearing about diabetes or what would happen if she didn't take her insulin.

I referred her to a social worker at the government social services office but I doubted that it would help. Shannon was determined to repeat the same cycle as her mother. I suggested counseling but she wasn't interested. I am certain we will see Shannon frequently until she dies from the complications of diabetes. Another little girl will be left motherless unnecessarily.

FACTS ABOUT DIABETES

Pathology

Six percent, or almost sixteen million Americans, have diabetes, another ten million are at risk for developing the disease. It is now considered an epidemic. The disease affects the body's ability to manage glucose (blood sugar). There are two forms of this disease that involve insulin, a hormone that helps the body store various nutrients in our cells.

Type 1 diabetes accounts for five to ten percent of all cases and develops most often in childhood. It is an auto-immune disease that destroys the body's ability to produce insulin.

Type 2 diabetes usually develops in adults and is caused by the body's inability to either make enough insulin or to effectively use the insulin it does make. It is diagnosed by a blood test which screens for elevated sugar levels.

Women can also develop Type 2 diabetes during pregnancy. This is called gestational diabetes. The risk of getting diabetes increases with age and obesity. African Americans, Hispanics, and American Indians have a higher incidence than Caucasians. Research has also shown that a lack of sleep over a long interval may contribute to the soaring incidence of diabetes in this country. Our hurried lifestyles and typical "American" diet are major suspects.

The following is a list of some of the symptoms that indicate that a physician should test you for diabetes:

Frequent urination

Extreme perception of thirst

Unexplained weight loss

Sudden vision changes

Tingling or numbness in fingers and toes

Extreme fatigue

Slow healing sores

Frequent infections

In the later stages of the disease certain other complications can result. These include high blood pressure, kidney failure, heart disease, decreased blood flow to the lower limbs that can result in amputations, blindness and even death. Most of these can be avoided with proper medical care.

Screening is automatically done during routine blood testing and should begin by age forty or sooner if another family member has the disease. Extra caution is need for those who are obese.

Type 1 diabetes is treated with daily insulin injections, exercise, and a restricted diet. Some people can use oral medicines to help reduce blood glucose levels.

Type 2 diabetes can be treated with exercise, diet, and either oral medications, insulin injections or both. However, one-third of those diagnosed with Type 2 diabetes don't get medical treatment. Many people don't realize they have the disease. Often, it is discovered only after an individual develops severe complications such as those described above.

Doctors report that even a little exercise and a diet change can delay the development of Type 2 diabetes. Medications to treat high blood pressure can delay and often prevent kidney failure in these patients.

There are new approaches being developed in the fight against this disease. Scientists are working on a pill that may alleviate the need for daily insulin shots. This could improve the quality of life for millions of diabetics who currently need daily shots to survive.

6

KIDNEY STONES

"The pain is horrible. I think I'm dying" "You've got to help me NOW!!!!"

Every day a few people arrive doubled over in pain, one hand on their lower back (left or right side) and standing on their tip-toes. To them, the pain seems unbearable. They are often loud and quite demanding of attention. They believe they are going to die at that very moment. After being assessed by a nurse at triage, they are referred back to the waiting room. Though it may feel like impending death, this situation is not considered critical and the wait may be hours. When they finally get to a treatment room, I find them doubled over in a tight fetal position. The patient can barely speak and wants to climb out of his or her own skin to escape the pain.

This pain often starts in the lower back on either side and moves to the front lower abdomen. If this is their first stone, patients believe they are suffering from appendicitis or a heart attack. They are extremely frightened.

Passing a kidney stone can be excruciating. I know. I have passed nine in the past ten years. The first one is the most frightening because the cause is unknown. Of course I imagined the worst. I suddenly felt as though a horse had kicked me in the lower back with immense force. Then, the horrible pain moved around towards the lower front of my abdomen. I became very nauseous and then proceeded to vomit more than a few times. At first, I, too, thought that I was having a heart attack. Then I was certain that my appendix was about to burst. I was terrified as I had never experienced so much pain before. It was 4:00 in the morning when I finally called my doctor. He told me to go to the emergency room if I couldn't wait until the next morning to see him. My temperature was normal so I decided to wait. What a long night it was. Nothing made the pain lessen. I spent one of my worst nights ever, doubled over in agony. I tried lying down, standing and even sitting but nothing helped. Those next five hours seemed like an eternity.

My doctor saw me first thing the next morning. Thank the

heavens! Blood was drawn and I was being x-rayed when the pain miraculously disappeared. I was very relieved when I was finally diagnosed. My father had kidney stones and I remember waking up many times in the middle of the night to his screams. My mother would hand him telephone books to tear up just to displace his pain while waiting for the ambulance to arrive. When my turn came, I did not connect the dots.

I now prepare myself for this by keeping a supply of pain pills on hand. When that familiar pain "punches me" in the lower back, I know just what it is. I begin to flush my kidneys by drinking as much water as fast as possible. I place a gallon of water beside me and lie down on the sofa to wait for the pain to pass. The stones take from six to eighteen hours to make their way through my system. The experience is much more pleasant (using the term loosely) if I am in my own home, watching television, rather than sitting in an emergency waiting room. However, I want to emphasize that if the pain persists, seek medical attention.

There are other treatments available and it is very important that your urine be checked for any signs of infection that can result from small cuts caused by the movement of the stone through the urinary tract.

FACTS ABOUT KIDNEY STONES

Kidney stones are one of the more common disorders that affect the urinary tract. It is estimated that one in ten people in the United States will have one at some point in their lives. It is more prevalent and more painful in men. Most kidney stones pass out of the body without any intervention by a doctor and often the stones are so small that we are unaware we are passing them. When this is not the case, sufferers come to the emergency room.

The kidneys are part of the urinary tract, which include the ureters, the bladder and the urethra. The kidneys are bean-shaped organs that are located below the ribs towards the middle of the back. Their purpose is to remove extra water and waste products from the blood and convert them to urine. The kidneys also help keep a stable balance of salts and other substances in the blood. Narrow tubes called ureters, carry the urine from the kidneys to the bladder. The bladder's elastic walls stretch, like a balloon, to store the urine. The urethra is a tube that extends from the bladder to allow urine to be eliminated from the body.

A kidney stone is a solid, microscopic piece of calcium or uric acid that literally slices its way through the ureter. The path is much narrower for males, which explains why it is exceedingly more painful for them. Although the pain is agonizing, there is little treatment available other than a shot of pain medication such as Demerol or Morphine and intravenous fluids to help flush out the kidneys. Time usually resolves the immediate problem. A urine sample is obtained to test for blood and infection. The stone usually passes within a matter of hours and, unless infection occurs, the pain miraculously disappears.

Kidney stones are made up of various chemicals found in a normal diet. Doctors don't know what causes stones to form; Scientists debate whether specific foods are at the root cause. They do know that a family history of kidney stones increases the likelihood. Urinary tract infections and kidney disorders also multiply the odds.

Some doctors recommend altering the diet to eliminate fruit

juices that contain high acid levels. Other doctors debate whether calcium-based stones are caused either by a shortage of calcium in the body, which the body then compensates for by stockpiling it, or an abundance of calcium, which causes the body to eliminate the excess. There are some doctors who do not believe that any dietary changes affect kidney stones.

In the past twenty years, the number of people diagnosed with kidney stones has increased. Statistics show that Caucasians are most susceptible to them. Kidney stones are most prevalent in people between the ages of twenty and forty. Once a kidney stone is discovered, it is likely that the problem will recur.

If kidney stones are diagnosed, the doctor will order a series of lab tests to measure the volume and levels of acid, calcium, sodium, uric acid, oxalate, citrate and creatine in the urine. The doctor will take a medical history and inquire about dietary habits to try to determine the cause of the stones. Drinking an adequate amount of water is the most important preventative measure. People prone to stones should drink at least two quarts of water every twenty-four hours. Those with calcified stones may need to eat fewer foods containing calcium and oxalate. Some may need additional calcium by taking certain antacids and added vitamin D. Diuretics can be prescribed to decrease the amount of calcium released by the kidneys.

If the stone does not pass within a reasonable amount of time, surgery may be needed. This is done if the patient remains in constant pain. Sometimes the stone is too large to pass on its own. Other times, the stone may block urine flow or cause constant bleeding and infection. The most frequently used procedure is ESWL or extracorporeal shockwave lithotripsy. The procedure uses shockwaves, generated by a device outside the body, to travel through the skin and body tissues until they pulverize the stones. The pulverized stones are like grains of sand and are flushed through the urinary tract via normal urination. This procedure can be done on either an inpatient and outpatient basis and is not painful.

7

DOMESTIC VIOLENCE

"but I love him"

I was ready to leave for the day when I got a call from Nurse Brenda to come to Station One immediately. The parents of Judy, a patient I had counseled earlier in the day, were waiting for me in the hall outside of Judy's room. Judy's case involved domestic violence and her story was an all too familiar one.

When I met Judy, she was thirty-one years old with an acne-scarred face and stringy, medium brown hair. She looked disheveled, her clothes were wrinkled, stained, and looked at least two sizes too big for her small frame. She had numerous tattoos on both forearms and one on her right ankle. Judy had a split lip and a swollen, bloodshot black eye from punches her boyfriend, Vince, had given her earlier in the day. Understandably, she was very upset. Judy told me that she had left their apartment to use the corner pay telephone to line up a drug "buy" for both of them. Vince punished her for not returning home "fast enough." Judy admitted that they were both "crack heads" but was quick to add that her boyfriend was violent only when under the influence. The problem was that he was ALWAYS under the influence. They had only been together for a few months and this was the fifth time he had assaulted her.

Judy said she was aware of the cycle of violence that was taking place but she felt incapable of pulling away from Vince permanently. She left him the last time that he had attacked her but she was not strong enough to stay away because she loved him so much. We spent quite a while together. Her spirit seemed broken. She believed she deserved no better than what she had now. We talked about domestic violence, safe shelters, and counseling but I feared that my words were falling on deaf ears.

It was many hours later and her parents were pleading with me to help get their daughter committed somewhere. Her parents were an ordinary, middle-class couple in their late fifties and they were desperate to save their daughter from the abuse. They were disheartened and dumfounded by the situation. They were also terrified that this abusive man would eventually beat their daughter to death.

Just two weeks before, Judy's parents had taken her back into their home after a similar trip to the hospital. She only stayed one night before returning again to Vince.

They were very angry that the police seemed to be so indifferent to Judy's plight. These were people who had lived their lives playing by "the rules" and now they needed some help and couldn't understand why it wasn't forthcoming. They wanted more effort put into apprehending the culprit and locking him away from their "little girl" before it was too late.

While I sympathized with their pain, I had to remind them that Judy was an adult and was free to make her own decisions, no matter how insane her choices might seem to others. All anyone could do for her, and other victims of domestic violence, was to encourage her to seek help. I explained that Judy's self-image was poor and that berating her would only make her feel less worthy of love and respect. Her parents told me that they could no longer bear witness to the abuse and they were too distraught to let Judy return home.

I gave her parents a copy of the laws and penalties for domestic violence infractions. I suggested that they go to the police and convince the authorities to pursue a criminal case against their daughter's abuser. There is punishment if the person is convicted. In fact, on the third conviction the perpetrator can be incarcerated for five years or more.

Earlier, I had given Judy a list of support services in the community. After talking with her parents, I decided to speak to Judy again. When I walked into her room she was curled up in a fetal position, hurt and angry that her parents had refused to allow her to return home. I asked her parents to come into Judy's room so that I could address all three of them together.

I asked Judy to turn and face us. She did so reluctantly. I reassured her that her parents and I cared about her because she was worth it and I wanted to "negotiate" an agreement among the three of them. Judy finally resolved to attend a minimum of five counseling sessions. With this promise, her parents agreed to take her home again, with the understanding that if she returned to Vince, they would never come to her rescue again.

Personally, I doubted that they would turn her away in the future. It was obvious to me just how much they loved their "baby."

After this interaction I couldn't wait to leave the hospital. Domestic violence cases disturb me greatly. So many wonderful women and men live with others who berate and beat on them. Every day is a living hell because the cycle of violence never ends. I am always dissatisfied that I am powerless to do more to help these people before they are seriously injured or killed.

One Time Too Many

I want to emphasize that people do die from domestic violence. One day a code was called on Tammy, a twenty-six year old woman who died at the hands of her husband. Tammy was a homemaker and the mother of three children, ranging in age from two to six. In the two years prior to her death, Tammy had come to the emergency room on five different occasions. Our medical team treated her and our social services team had given her the usual advice and lists of the available support resources in the community. She even pressed charges once; but when her husband was released from jail, he beat her so viciously that she nearly died then. I had no prior interaction with Tammy, so I was not as upset as the other staff members who knew her. They were visibly shaken by her death.

I was the one selected to meet with her family and help them sort it all out. Her brother, a strapping young man with a bulky physique and large, meaty arms, looked like a construction worker. When I entered Tammy's room, he was leaning forward in the chair, head resting between his immense hands and he was sobbing uncontrollably. Overpowered by grief and guilt, he was totally devastated by his "big" sister's early death. He regretted not killing Tammy's husband when he was first released from jail.

Her brother told me that on the night of her death, the police had been called to Tammy's apartment by a neighbor who heard screaming. When the police arrived, they found her husband in front of the television set playing video games while Tammy laid unconscious and bleeding in their bedroom. Her husband was immediately taken into custody and was later charged with murder but that was of little comfort to Tammy's loved ones. Domestic violence destroyed their entire family.

Many victims of domestic violence arrive at the emergency room bloody and battered. Domestic violence is defined as a pattern of assaultive behaviors that one person uses to control another in a relationship. These acts may include physical, emotional, sexual, economic and psychological abuse.

Domestic violence involves a husband and wife, a boyfriend and girlfriend, same-sex partners, parents and their children and children against children. Untold horrors permeate the very core of our society. Many thousands die each year from domestic violence abuse; Others continue to live in a war zone in their own homes, behind closed doors. Terrified to leave and even more frightened to remain, these beaten victims show up with contusions, bruises, broken bones and crushed spirits. I witness society's inhumanity daily and I hate it!

Cricket

Child abuse is also a part of the cycle of domestic violence. Many young and abused girls grow up to become prostitutes. They also have a high incidence of drug addiction. The cycle repeats itself and more lives are shattered for generations to come.

One memorable day brought all this into perspective for me. It was the middle of my shift and I was making rounds. When I arrived at Station Three, I was asked to meet with a 22 year-old methamphetamine addict. Cricket was admitted to the ER after being severely beaten by her pimp. She desperately needed domestic violence counseling and support. I already knew I would be frustrated before I spoke with her. So many victims return to their abusive situations because they have been brainwashed into believing they do not deserve any better. Worse, many of these victims are afraid of what will happen if they do leave, since the period right after leaving the abuser is the most dangerous time. The victims realize that the abuser's threats are real and their promises to kill may be carried out. Many remain with their abuser, honestly believing it will be safer for them and their families.

I was struck by Cricket's youthful appearance. Although twenty-two years-old, she could have easily passed for a teenager. She was barely five feet tall, ninety-five pounds. Her hair was shoulder length, light brown and curly, and matted from all the dried blood. Her clothing was torn and bloody, too.

Cricket was lying on her right side in a fetal position with the sheet pulled up around her neck. There was an intra-venous tube protruding from her right hand. Her left arm was in a cast and her left leg had been broken in two places. I quietly entered her room and gently asked, "Hi Cricket. Are you awake?" She sobbed softly. I continued, "My name is Marsha and I am the social worker here in the emergency room. Can we talk?" She slowly nodded so I got closer. I pulled up a chair next to her bed. She turned toward me and I saw her blackened left eye and she had three large cuts on her cheeks. Her lips were so swollen that it was difficult for her to close her mouth.

"I am so sorry this happened to you. Will you tell me about it?" I really wanted to hear her story.

Cricket was numb from the painkillers and she could only mumble. Tears were streaming down her face and her little body heaved under the covers. I thought my heart would break in two. She was somebody's daughter, somebody's sister, maybe even a mother herself. This little woman, a novice in the world, was careening on a path of self-destruction before her life had even begun to unfold. I just sat there in silence for what seemed like an eternity. I finally reached out and gently touched her shoulder. In a soft voice, I assured her that she was safe, that she should rest and I promised her that I would return soon.

I left her room feeling so much sadness. What could I possibly say that would make a difference in her life? How could I, a stranger, motivate her enough to save her own life before it was too late?

I walked outside to get some fresh air and to plan what I would do with Cricket. My heart felt heavy, my breathing was labored and my eyes were filled with tears. I reflected on my own life and how I could have become another Cricket.

My own childhood was filled with abuse and rage. My parents were always angry about something and love and support were rare. I grew up believing that I was ugly and skinny and had no value. My parents let me know that I was "lucky" they were "willing" to even feed me, much less take care of me. I left home at sixteen and with little self-esteem, I turned to drugs to mask my pain. I lived in a world of violence, witnessed deaths from drug overdoses and soon, I just didn't care what happened to me.

After a number of attempts to recover on my own, I entered a drug rehabilitation program and, at age 17, met a wonderful woman named June. She was a volunteer there and though the same age as my mother, she was kind and loving and spent many hours talking with me. With her love and support, I developed a sense of my self and began to believe that I deserved more. She and her husband had offered me a place to live if I ever wanted to get my life on track. I wasn't ready yet.

Six months passed. Then, one day, ill, dehydrated, emaciated, and in the throes of withdrawal, I hitchhiked thirty miles to their home and fell into June's arms, begging for help. That was the turning point for me. I threw up often and I slept fourteen hours or more a day. This was the first time I had felt loved and valued. June spent most of my waking hours telling me know how much potential I had and how deeply she cared for and about me.

I remained in June's home for six months. She taught me to care about myself through her example. I continued to grow and change and never looked back to those dark days again.

I stood outside the hospital reflecting on all of those memories. How could I be a stepping stone for Cricket? How could I plant just one seed in her that would make a difference? Unlike June, I only had a few hours to make an impact. What could I say to let her know that I cared about her and more importantly, that she was worth caring about? Hospital policy would not allow me to offer my home and hospitality to Cricket. I understood that policy and also knew that I could never bring drugs and violence back into my life. I just needed faith that the right words would come to me.

Two hours later, I went back to Cricket's room. This time she was awake. The pain medication was beginning to fade and her pain was terrible. I poked my head in the door. "Hi," I said in as cheerful a voice as I could manage, "Remember me? " Cricket blinked her eyes and I took a seat about two feet from her bed. I looked into her sad, hollow blue eyes and her drawn face; then at the needle tracks in her forearms and the thin black lines that marked a permanent road map to her years of self-abuse. I wondered, could she really be only twenty-two years old? So much horror in such a short period of time.

"Can you tell with me what happened?" I asked. "Maybe I can help."

She started to cry as she told me how her boyfriend/pimp woke her up, and demanded that she get out of bed and head out to the streets so they would have money to buy more drugs.

As she tried to wake up, her boyfriend began beating her with his fists. He punched her in the face, screaming that she was an ugly, worthless whore. "Why does he hate me so much?" she sobbed, "I was moving as fast as I could, but I couldn't get out of his way." The boyfriend then jumped on her arm and leg until there was a snap and she couldn't move. He then dragged Cricket outside by the hair and left her on the sidewalk.

"How did you get to the hospital?" I asked. She replied that someone was walking by and asked if she needed an ambulance. For a moment I actually felt relieved and grateful that a complete stranger had cared enough to help. "Did he ask how you were doing or offer to stay until the paramedics arrived?" "No." she stated in a matter-of-fact tone. "He just kept on walking. At least he called an ambulance for me." My heart sank. How often we all walk around oblivious to the pain and suffering of others. Cricket was not surprised that the stranger left her broken and in misery. She expected no help from others. She trusted no one, not even herself.

Cricket talked about her childhood, complete with incidents of sexual abuse by her stepfather beginning at age eight. Her mother was an alcoholic and was unable to protect her from him. She lived in constant fear. Crickett ran away from home at the age of sixteen. She arrived in Las Vegas with five dollars in her pocket and turned to prostitution to earn money to buy food.

The third day in town, she met her pimp, Ben, who offered her a place to stay, food to eat and a false sense of security. He was abusive right from the beginning. Cricket attempted to leave Ben many times, but as the cycle of violence continued, he would find her, apologize, then start abusing her again.

I asked her if she wanted to press assault charges and she said no. I was not surprised. In the State of Nevada, as well as many other states, the law does not require the victim to press charges. However, Nevada Law does require a peace officer to arrest a person if the officer has probable cause to believe that the person has, within the preceding 24 hours, committed a battery against his spouse, former spouse or any other person he is related to by blood or marriage (NRS 171.37). Also, the law specifies that the officer's decision to make an arrest must not be made on the officer's perception of the victim, her unwillingness to testify or participate in judicial matters. That sounds good but I have seen it rarely used.

Cricket and I spent two hours together. She agreed to move in with a friend but remained too frightened to press charges and too psychologically immobilized to leave the city.

After her release from the emergency room, I called a cab, escorted her out of the hospital and gave her my card. I did my best to convince her that she was a worthwhile person, that life could be better, and that she was entitled to as much happiness as anyone else. I assured her that if she wanted my help in the future, I would do everything I could for her.

I gently hugged her goodbye and watched as she got into the cab that took her away. My spirit was very injured. I felt such sorrow then. I still do. I can only pray that some day she will reach out and accept help.

FACTS ABOUT DOMESTIC VIOLENCE

Domestic violence is an epidemic that cuts across all classes of society, culture, race, and gender. Ninety-five percent of the victims are female. It may involve a friend, co-worker or neighbor.

Domestic violence may seem benign at first but it will surely escalate. Initially, the abuser may resort to name calling or destroying the personal property or sentimental items of the victim. The victim may be pushed, shoved, hit, slapped, grabbed, bitten, kicked, choked, or even burned. The abuse escalates to death threats, beatings and intimidation with weapons. It often ends in death.

More police are injured or killed intervening in these situations than all other cases combined. Victims are afraid to involve the police because penalties are light and the repercussions can be fatal. Victims often return to the abusive relationship after their abuser is released from jail. It takes an average of seven to ten attempts before the victim actually leaves their abuser for good.

All jurisdictions in the United States have implemented the Violence Against Women Act, signed into law by President Clinton in 1994. This law makes domestic violence a civil rights violation and was designed to protect victims of domestic violence and to strengthen prevention and increase the penalties for violent crimes against women and children. The Violence Against Women Act strengthened and expanded the protections of federal and state laws.

There are shelters available in undisclosed locations for the protection of victims and children. Toll-free hotlines offer support and direction to other resources. Information is available at police departments, mental health agencies and at all hospitals.

IDENTIFYING AN ABUSER

Batterers and abusive people demonstrate certain identifiable behaviors. Remember that all forms of physical, psychological, and economic abuse come from the abuser's need to control and a desire for power. The following is a list to help you recognize if someone you know or love is in a violent situation.

1. Is there name calling, put-downs, accusations, blaming, yelling, swearing, humiliating remarks or gestures?

2. Is there pressure to make decisions inconsistent with the values and desires of those making them?

3. Is there guilt or other forms of intimidation? Is money withheld? Are they told what to do?

4. Does the abuser always have to be right? Do they interrupt, change topics, twist words and demean their partner in front of other friends and family members?

5. Are promises broken constantly? Do they refuse to help with child care and housework?

6. Does the abuser not express feelings? Does the abuser refuse to give support, attention or compliments?

7. Does the batterer not take others' feelings seriously?

8. Does he interfere with the victim's sense of economic security by calling too often at work and making unwanted personal visits? Does he hide the car keys to prevent the victim from going to work?

9. Is the victim prevented from seeing friends or relatives? Are telephone calls monitored?

10. Are personal and sentimental belongings of others destroyed?

11. Is she forced into performing sexual acts against her will?

12. Does the abuser make threats or carry out threats to the victim? Do they drive recklessly or use physical size to intimidate?

This is just a short list of warning signs that often lead up to physical violence. Physical violence can also entail being violent to household pets, children or others outside of the home.

It is an escalating cycle that often ends in the incarceration of the offender and too often, the death of the victim. If someone is in this situation, help them create the foundation to leave. Have an emergency plan prepared in advance. The plan should include the following:

- Have an escape route planned ahead of time.

- Make certain there is a way to call 911.

- Teach the children to dial the police.

- Pack a bag with clothes, money, spare keys and identification and keep it in a safe place with family or with friends.

Plan a safe and secret place to go. This can be a motel, a friend's house or a shelter. Make certain that the abuser does not know where the safe place is located.

Maintain a list of important telephone numbers at all times. Include police, shelters, counselors, relatives and friends. Find out the toll-free number for the hot line in your area. Call them for support and direction.

There are resources available in all our communities that are specifically designed to assist the victim to escape the horror happening in their own home.

Many victims feel overwhelmed and powerless to help themselves until it is too late. If you think you know of someone trapped in a similar nightmare, reach out. Offer your assistance. Don't be discouraged if they return to their abuser the first few times. Domestic violence is a disease that grabs onto its victims until they don't have the emotional fortitude to do anything about it. They need our help.

8

THE HOMELESS

"I am not like <u>those</u> people"

Every day we encounter five or more homeless men and women in the emergency room. They often arrive by ambulance since they don't have the money for any public form of transportation. The faces are all too familiar. Their hair is full of oil and dirt. The stench from their body and clothes just can't be adequately described. Many of the homeless have not showered for years and often wear the same unwashed clothing for months at a time. They rarely have ready access to the proper items to wipe and wash after relieving themselves. Their body odor permeates the entire emergency room and attacks everyone's sense of smell that is within range. It is unmistakable. Nothing can kill this foul smell. When I started working there, I would get nauseous whenever I encountered it.

The homeless often appear tired and haggard, looking

decades older than their chronological ages would indicate. Their skin is leathery and wrinkled, their bodies frail with their histories written on their faces like a textbook on how to grow old rapidly and without grace.

They are usually dehydrated, dizzy, hungry and just plain exhausted from the journey to nowhere. The smell of stale alcohol permeates the room. Most have seizures from too many years of self-abuse. We put them in hospital garbs, fill them with medications, give them sandwiches, and allow them a few hours of sleep.

"Hey, Marsha, there's one waiting to see you." one of the staff members announces as I walk by. "Thanks a lot." I silently reply, knowing that it will be useless to attempt any interaction until they awake hours later.

Because our hospital receives federal funding, we have to treat everyone who says they have a medical problem. Too often, the homeless fill up our beds and waiting rooms even though they may need no medical intervention.

It is extremely frustrating to keep the sick and injured waiting hours for care while our beds fill up with non-medical cases. Many of the staff resent working with these patients. At first I didn't understand why my co-workers had such little compassion for the homeless and addicted. Then I began to feel that way too. It is frustrating to provide care for those who don't care about themselves. Many have given up on life. They often don't have dreams or goals for the future and the daily struggle to survive another day defines the scope of their horizon. They are often delirious and can become violent without provocation and need to be restrained.

I continue to try to reach out to them because every so often, I get a renewed sense of hope when I meet someone like John.

GOOD TIMES, BAD TIMES......

John was fifty-nine. His face was red and bloated face from years of drinking. The capillaries on his nose and upper cheeks were quite pronounced. He initially came in because his diabetes was out of control which caused his feet to become black and swollen. His nurse said he had been quite boisterous and demanding. She asked me to intervene and to quiet him down. I walked by his room and poked my head in to see him. He was lying face up on a gurney. "Hi John, my name is Marsha. I'm the social worker here. Mind if I come in?"

His gaze followed my movements though he would not make direct eye contact. "Sure, come on in." he replied in a hostile tone of voice. I shook his hand and pulled up a chair. I began asking him questions about his present situation and how he ended up without a home.

John relayed his story in minute detail. He was angry and bitter at first. He believed that the "system" had done him wrong. He couldn't find a job and his life "stunk." I listened without expressing any judgments and let him continue. His demeanor softened within ten minutes and I began to care about him.

Almost twenty years ago, John had been a very successful businessman with a wife and a son he dearly loved. While in Algiers on a work assignment, his wife was killed by a bomb that was detonated in the Algiers airport. At first, I thought he was making up the story, but then I remembered the incident as it had been widely reported in the news.

John was devastated by the event. He had been standing

next to his wife when the bomb exploded and he watched her body disintegrate into millions of pieces. He had been seriously injured in the attack and had spent two weeks in the hospital recovering from shrapnel fragments and a broken pelvis.

John returned to the United States a broken man. His business collapsed. He couldn't concentrate and depression took over his life. Six months after that horrible event, his seventeen year-old son committed suicide by putting a shotgun in his mouth and pulling the trigger. John lost his final reason for living.

After the death of his son, he drank himself into a daily stupor. He quickly lost his home, his car and his friends. For more than five years, John drifted from one part-time, low-paying menial job, to another.

Gradually, John's life began anew. He managed to get a job in engineering again and invented a system to reduce production costs on assembly lines for computers. He sold his ideas to a major player in the industry. Soon, John was earning a six-figure salary again and had a home, a car, and all the material possessions he wanted. Then, he met and married a woman much younger than himself. He was back in the game of life.

Two years later there was a new crisis. His wife left him and took most of his money. This incident destroyed his new found self-esteem. He began to drink again and within a few short months he was back on the streets, living out of the bottom of a bottle.

He never recuperated from that last blow. Sometimes he was able to earn enough to stay in a run-down hotel on Fremont Street in downtown Las Vegas. He started to cry as he shared his life with me. I felt privileged that he was willing to open up and reveal his innermost feelings. John truly believed that he did not deserve any more breaks. He only lived to drink himself to death. He had no possessions, no one to care about and no one who cared about him. I asked if he had ever been in counseling, even though men of his generation usually don't go for psychiatric treatment. He said he had attended Alcoholics Anonymous meetings many times in the past, but saw no reason to continue trying.

I tried to reassure John and to encourage him to try again. I suggested a shelter, therapy, and part-time employment, but he just wasn't interested. He only wanted medical treatment so he could walk comfortably to the nearest liquor store.

I saw John later that day as he was putting his dirty clothes back on and preparing to leave the hospital. There was something different about his demeanor. He was standing tall, had combed his hair, and was walking lighter. He looked directly at me and smiled. I knew that we both felt good about our interaction. I can only hope he will try again.

FRUSTRATION

I walked into room 34 to find a sixty-two year-old man dressed in a hospital gown, a large-brimmed straw cowboy hat and sunglasses. He was diagnosed with an advanced case of diabetes. He needed dialysis right away. His legs were swollen to at least four times their normal size. He insisted that he was worth four million dollars from a trust fund set up by his parents years earlier. I seriously doubted that he was worth four million dollars or even four hundred, for that matter. Sent to us from a total-care facility, he was angry, loud and unmanageable.

"Everyone is stealing from me." he complained after I introduced myself. "My wheelchair and my cigarettes are missing. The staff at the "home" ignore me so I have to pee in the bed." He continued his tirade. "I had two girlfriends. I was going to live with them but they both dumped me at the hospital when I wouldn't sign over my power-of-attorney to them. I can't believe they only want me for my money."

I just listened as he vented. He refused our offer of medical treatment. He just wanted to complain about his love life, or lack thereof. He was driving his nurse and the surrounding patients, to distraction. I was asked to try to get him to reconsider medication. I tried but it didn't work. He continued his belligerent ways for two hours.

The doctor finally admitted defeat and instructed his nurse to write up the discharge papers. I offered him a free taxi ride to a homeless shelter or to another nursing home since he had worn out his welcome at the last place. I also offered to make arrangements for him to move back to his home state of Ohio. I suggested that he should rent an apartment and hire a private nurse if he could afford one. He refused to even consider it. He continued to insist that all he needed was a young woman who would take care of him out of love. No other options would do.

His medical and psychological problems made him a huge responsibility to anyone wanting to help. I felt somewhat sympathetic, but after much irritation and frustration, I gave up trying to reach him. I just couldn't get through his delusional system. I ended up escorting him to the taxi pick-up area and sent him on a one way trip to the Salvation Army. His situation was unchanged, and unfortunately, I knew we had not seen the last of him.

THE HOMELESS PROBLEM IN LAS VEGAS

The homeless problem in Las Vegas is extensive, probably more so than in most other metropolitan areas. For the hard-core street people, the weather is better for sleeping outside and there are a number of shelters and homeless centers available during bad weather. Many working poor come to Las Vegas with high hopes of obtaining good paying jobs in the glamorous casino industry. What many people don't realize is that there are strict rules and an unusually large number of regulations to be met before most employers can hire someone. Police-issued work cards are required prior to becoming employed in a casino or any establishment associated with gaming, regardless of the position. Also, without prior experience in casino work, first-time employees are often put on a "callboard." A callboard is a list of potential temporary employees who are called for any shift on any day to fill in for full-time employees. Call board employees usually work part-time. Frequently, it is the only way that many people can work their way into a full-time job.

There are also barriers to becoming a taxi driver or security guard in the form of licensing costs that must be paid up front. After the events of September 11, 2001, the unemployment rate increased dramatically and jobs had become scarce. Unprepared for all the employment delays, many gamble away what little money they arrive with. They quickly join the ranks of the homeless.

The homeless have a culture of sorts. They share information on services and how to manipulate the various government agencies. They know what hospitals will be the kindest and the fastest and what to say to stay as long as possible. One summer we admitted six men within a week for blisters on the bottoms of their feet. They had deliberately walked barefoot for two hours on the hot pavement. Self-inflicted pain bought them about eighteen hours in the hospital with; food, water, air conditioning, a clean comfortable bed, and color TV.

Any individual only needs to say he requires medical care to receive it.

9

DRUG OVERDOSES

'It was only prescription medication"

Mother's Day was extremely busy during my entire shift. It was obvious that many of the nurses were doing their jobs but their hearts weren't in it. Since I have no family locally, I try to get assigned to work holidays whenever possible. I knew I was needed as the waiting room remained full throughout my shift.

It was 3:00 in the afternoon when the ambulance roared in with its lights flashing. It was a "code" and all of the medical staff scrambled to room seven to prepare. Life and death could hinge on everyone's actions in the next few minutes. Tension ran high as the emergency equipment was pushed into the room. The patient was a young Caucasian male, age thirty, rushed in on a gurney with an intravenous tube already inserted into his left arm. His skin was a grayish tinge and he was struggling to breathe. His heart stopped as they were lifting him into his hospital bed. Crews ripped his cowboy-studded denim shirt open so that shock paddles could be placed directly on his chest. CPR was started. He was revived and the breathing tube was inserted down his throat. I noticed this man took great pride in his personal appearance. His muscles were buffed just enough to make him look quite masculine but not overdone. He was very attractive with a slight mustache and sandy brown, close-cropped hair.

"What happened?" I asked. It did not make sense to see such a young, healthy-looking male "coding" on the table. "He took a huge overdose of percodan with a fifth of vodka." the paramedic told me. "His roommate found him slumped over the bed when he got home from work. There were at least thirty pills missing from the prescription bottle that had been filled at the local pharmacy yesterday." At this point, a tube was inserted down the patient's nose and into his stomach and liquid charcoal was pushed down the tubing. This was done to absorb the toxins in his stomach. After that, the stomach contents were suctioned out and began to fill the plastic container attached to the end of the tube, which was resting off to one side of the bed. One pill became visible and this process continued until at least twenty-five little yellow pills appeared. By now the patient was in a coma and no one knew if he would ever regain consciousness.

As they inserted more tubes he began to look like the bionic man. One nurse inserted a catheter into his penis so his body could release urine automatically. All poisons had to be removed from his body before too much was absorbed into his bloodstream. At the same time, other nurses were inserting intravenous tubes into his arms in order to inject fluids and medications into his body rapidly.

This was the first code I had ever witnessed and I watched in awe and horror. "What could have possibly been so bad for this young man to do this to himself?" I wondered. "It's Mother's Day. Please God. Don't make me have to call his mother and tell her that her son is dead; Not today." I found out his name was Paul. I spent much of my day with him and I talked to him even though he couldn't respond. I had no way of knowing if he even heard me. Some patients recall conversations after they come out of comas, others do not. (I choose to believe that they all hear me.) The sense of hearing is the last one to shut down so I kept trying. I sat in his room and touched his arm frequently.

I was angry with him for having done such a dumb thing. "How could he be so selfish?" I thought to myself. "Was he trying to punish someone else; Was he trying to get someone's attention?" I had many emotions all wrapped up in a ball in the pit of my stomach. I would check on him frequently and I drove his nurse to distraction with my constant questions.

Hours passed with no change in his condition. We had no way of knowing how much had been absorbed into his system, and if he did awaken, what damage had been done to his body and his mind. All we could do was wait. I wiggled his toes, poked him, shook him and demanded, "Wake up, damn it. I don't want you to die!"

Three hours later, I decided to try again. "Wake up! Wake up, Paul!" Again, I began shaking his foot. Suddenly his eyes opened. He looked totally shocked to see me standing over him. He did not know where he was or what had happened. I leaned closer to him. "Hi. Welcome back. You're in a hospital and came about as close as anyone could to killing yourself."

He tried to talk and then he realized that he couldn't utter a sound as he still had the breathing tube down his throat. I noticed how beautiful his eyes were. I was happy that he woke up but soon I found my anger returning. I wanted to trick him into believing that he had succeeded and was now in Hell. It must have seemed that way to him already with the tubes down his throat and nose, the catheter in his penis and the intravenous lines running fluid into both arms. His hands were tied down to either side of the bed to prevent movement.

I called out to his nurse to let her know that Paul had woken up. I left him for a short while to deal with another situation. What a day; One crisis after another. A short time later, I was able to return to talk with Paul again. He was able to breath on his own so the breathing tube had been removed. He claimed that the overdose was an accident. He protested that he had gotten careless with the pills and after a time, was so high that he didn't realize how many pills he had ingested. I reminded him that it was Mother's Day. "Do you hate your mother?" I asked. "No." he sheepishly replied. "I love her very much." "Well, wouldn't it have just made her day if I had to call her today to tell her that her son was dead?" He didn't answer me. Instead, he seemed embarrassed and ashamed of what had transpired. He shared with me that he had been partying way too much lately. I suggested some services so he could get help with his addictions and personal problems. My last words to him were "Call your mother, today!"

Drug Addiction
It's Everyone else's fault!

Since that day, I have witnessed far too many mothers, father, wives, husbands, and children, sitting vigil, praying that their loved ones did not die from drug overdoses. It always breaks my heart. Some are angry and share one frustrating incident after another. Many have reached out to others for assistance including law enforcement, therapists, friends and family. They have tried tough love, avoidance and pleading. Nothing has helped for long.

One mother actually begged me to write a letter to help her son avoid going back to prison for another two years after a parole violation. His mother had bailed him out of jail the night before and he had talked her into giving him some spending money. He used it to buy drugs. Now he was in the emergency room because of an overdose. She told me "I have not had a happy day since Matt began using drugs nineteen years ago. If only his wife hadn't left him, he would be okay." I was stunned at her denial about Matt's problem. Matt was forty-three years old and had never held a job for longer than three weeks. He had stolen thousands of dollars from his family, ruined his mother's credit, alienated the rest of his family and created chaos in his own life. I asked if she had other children and how they were doing. She finally smiled. "Fine. All my kids turned out well except Matt." "Do you have happy times with them?" I wanted to understand the family dynamics. "No, she replied. I am always worried about Matt. My husband keeps threatening to leave me if I don't stop giving in to him but I don't know what else to do."

I felt sad for the rest of the family as well. The other children

Date Rape

Some drug overdoses are suicide attempts. Other cases are due to carelessness. Tonight we had an overdose that was part of a rape and robbery. Amy's case illustrates this scenario. Amy and three friends flew to Las Vegas from Oregon to help her celebrate her twenty-first birthday. After unpacking, the group decided to go out to one of the best nightclubs in town. While partying on the dance floor, someone had slipped a tablet of GHB, also known as Ecstasy, into Amy's drink. The night would end with Amy arriving at the emergency room by ambulance.

After she was admitted, I was called in to assess her mental condition. Amy did not know her name, where she was, the day of the week, the year or who was the current President of the United States. Her eyes were glazed over and she was very frightened. Her hands were trembling and she could not stop crying. She knew something was horribly wrong but was too intoxicated to focus for more than a few minutes. Amy quickly fell back asleep, so I left her room.

Two hours later, I returned to find a completely different woman. Amy was back in the present and could remember everything that had happened up to the point of finishing her drink. After that, time was a blank. She remembered waking up outside of an abandoned building in the most dangerous part of town. A Good Samaritan had spotted her lying on the ground and called an ambulance from his cell phone. She was rushed to the hospital.

Amy was given a rape exam and her blood was tested for venereal and other infectious disease. She was extremely fortunate. All the tests came back negative although she would need to be tested again within the next six months to be certain. She survived what could have been her last party.

Amy was released later that day and emphatically told me that she was heading right back home to Portland on the next available flight. I was sorry that her celebration had turned out so badly. I do believe she will be very careful in bars and nightclubs in the future. Drug overdoses can happen to anyone, whether or not they willingly take them.

Shelly, age eighteen, was not so lucky. According to her

parents, Shelly had attended a party two days before her arrival to the emergency room. Shelly had come home around two in the morning and had gone directly to bed. Her mother heard her stumbling around the house and assumed that Shelly had too much to drink but she would just sleep it off. The next morning her parents could not awaken her. In a panic, they called 911 and Shelly was rushed to the emergency room by ambulance.

Our medical team could not revive her either. She was given intravenous medications to dilute and flush the unknown chemicals from her body. She was intubated to help her breathe. Blood was taken to try to determine what drug had put her into this state of unconsciousness. Shelly remained in the ER for twelve hours with no sign of improvement. She was moved to a room in the Intensive Care Unit. When I checked on her weeks later, I was told she had been transferred to a long-term care facility where she remained in a coma. I don't know if someone had put drugs into Shelly's drink or if she took them willingly. All I knew was that at the age of eighteen her life looked finished, unless by some miracle, she recovered.

THE BLUE PEOPLE

Are there aliens in the ER?

I had only been at work a half an hour when I glanced over to room seven. I observed a very old woman lying in bed, fully "tubed." I did an instant double take when I realized that she had blue skin. It was not the shade of blue that one gets when cold or dehydrated but it was almost a deep sky blue. She already looked dead, and worse, but her chest was moving up and down and the machines were still assisting her. I immediately walked over to the doctor and asked him what was wrong with her. The doctor shook his head and replied, "Go look at her husband. He's the same color. He won't talk to any of us. See if he'll speak with you."

I walked back into her room and was startled to find a large-framed man about the same age as the patient, sitting in the corner. Other than his blue skin color, he looked fit and healthy. He was wearing scruffy blue jeans and a red and black plaid shirt, with large brown boots that were worn and covered with dried mud. I hid my shock and introduced myself. He was open and receptive. We chit-chatted for a few minutes so I pulled over a chair and sat down.

"What's wrong with your wife?" I inquired innocently, my mind was racing with crazy thoughts. They both looked like aliens that had landed a little off-course from Area 51, the famous UFO spot 45 miles outside of Las Vegas. "We've been melting down 99 9/10 proof silver to a liquid form and drinking it." he answered. I was stunned and asked him why they would drink liquid metal. "Because it is a homeopathic treatment for infections." he calmly shrugged his shoulders and replied. "Are you aware that you both have turned blue?" I asked as nonchalantly as possible while trying to keep a straight face. He smiled. "Yes, I know that but it's easier to overdose on regular medicine than herbal treatments. I don't believe in doctors and modern medicine." he emphatically stated. He was absolutely confident that his beliefs were correct. He then told me that his wife was a diabetic and he did not believe in insulin so after her last hospitalization, he took her off of insulin and treated her with this silver drink instead.

I couldn't take my eyes off of him. I wondered if either one of them could make it through a metal detector without sounding the alarms. If they were cremated, would there be a puddle of silver left when all else had turned to ash? I was astonished that someone would turn blue and still believe he was living a healthy life. They were both from the mid-west and spent most of their lives together on a small farm with little outside contact. He totally believed he was healing his wife's condition. His fear of modern medicine and doctors were killing them both.

His wife was close to death. She went in and out of consciousness and her mouth remained partly open all the time. She reminded me of a fish in a half-filled aquarium. Her nose was covered by an oxygen mask, giving her the look of a science fiction character. Her white hair was unkempt and bluish; her eyes were deep in their sockets. I tried to speak with her but she did not seem to hear me. Her husband wasn't the least bit worried. He was certain that his "treatment" was appropriate and that she would be well in a few days.

I excused myself and promised to return soon. I located her doctor to share my newly-acquired information. He added that the patient was suffering from metal poisoning and that this was the worst case he had ever seen. I asked if I should call in senior protective services since her "treatments" were killing her. "Does she need protection from him?" "Don't bother." he replied. "She'll die soon." I checked on her a few more times and then moved on to other cases. All of the staff were talking about the blue people. One by one, they walked by just to see them.

An hour later, I heard a Code 99 being called over the intercom system for room W228. I asked the charge nurse if that was the blue woman's new room. The charge nurse recognized the number immediately. When the patient was taken upstairs to the critical care unit, a nurse had walked by, saw the patient, and assumed she was dead. The emergency room nurse called upstairs to assure them that the patient was stable and definitely still alive. I knew that it was just a matter of time before she wouldn't be.

10

Miscarriages

'Hurry! I'm losing my baby"

I was helping out in the triage office when a young woman showed up at the window weeping and holding her abdomen. Her small frame shook with each sob. I walked out of the office and over to where she was sitting. She proceeded to tell me that she was eight weeks pregnant and was petrified that she was having a miscarriage. She had been experiencing severe cramping and vaginal bleeding for the past few hours. I asked her to take a seat, fill out the necessary short form, and said we would get to her as soon as possible. It was a hectic day and the waiting time would be long.

Ten minutes later I looked up and observed her bent over the chair, head on her knees, wincing with pain. Immediately my heart went out to her, so I decided to approach her in an attempt to ease her fears. Kim told me that she was twenty-five years old and married. She had been trying to get pregnant for three years. She and her husband were ecstatic when the home pregnancy test was positive. Her parents were thrilled at the prospect of having a new grandchild. This was a much wanted baby.

Kim started bleeding while her husband was at work and she did not want to upset him so she drove herself to the hospital. She was terrified and so alone with her pain and fear. I took her to an office away from the waiting room so we could speak in private. I said "I am really sorry that this is happening to you. You must be very frightened." I wanted her to know that this was not necessarily due to any wrong-doing on her part. I said, "Up to thirty percent of all pregnancies end in a miscarriage during the first three months. Unfortunately, there is little doctors can do to stop the process. They do not fully understand why this occurs but many surmise that it is nature taking over due to a genetic defect of some kind. The end result is determined by a much higher power." I explained this to relieve Kim's sense of urgency and ease any regrets about not coming to the emergency room sooner.

Once she was taken to the treatment area, the doctor gave her a gynecological examination and ordered blood tests and an ultrasound of her abdomen. (I always try to accompany the doctor when he tells the patient the results especially if the fetus is no longer viable). Kim was told that she was no longer pregnant. She was devastated. The doctor explained to her that this baby just wasn't meant to be, for whatever reason. He left the room quickly but I stayed to talk to her about her feelings. She needed to grieve the loss of her baby and her plans and dreams for it.

While there are some advantages to home pregnancy tests, there is also a down side. Before self-administered tests were available over-the-counter, women waited three months before getting tested. There was less chance of miscarriage and the doctor was present to give the results and handle the initial emotional reaction. In the "olden days", a missed period was perceived as a possible pregnancy but when the period arrived the next month, although heavy, it wasn't given much thought. The home tests can be accurate if taken three days before the next period begins. This means that the fetus is less than thirty days old and is still quite fragile. The test and the outcome are known within minutes. Good news or bad, the emotions go into over-drive immediately.

If the baby is wanted, its future begins at the moment the results are known. When a miscarriage occurs, the parents are left with broken hearts and shattered dreams. Friends and loved ones mean well but the worst thing to say at that moment is, "Don't worry. You can try again." While this is probably true, that statement does not lessen the pain nor does it deal with the grief the parents feel for the child that will never be born.

I asked Kim about her marriage and if she wanted my assistance with telling Mark about the loss of their baby. She wanted to wait a while to process the information and prepare for his reaction.

I returned a half-hour later to ask if she was ready. She said she now felt strong enough to speak with him so I dialed the number and handed her the phone. She asked him to meet her at the hospital without sharing the news. She wanted to tell him in person and requested that I be there with her when she shared the bad news. She promised to have me paged when he arrived.

An hour later Nurse Valerie told me that Kim wanted to see me. She had already revealed the news to him before I returned. I was pleased to find Kim and her husband crying together in each other's arms. The three of us talked for a short while and I left them alone. I had no doubt that they would be fine and when the time came, they would make terrific parents. I knew that they would never forget the child that didn't survive.

Grieving over a miscarriage can take a long time but it needs to happen to empower the parents to move beyond this tragedy. The best thing anyone can do to help is to just listen without judgments, excuses or rationalizations. It is a big deal and not something to you "get over" quickly. I try to get the partners started on the process by helping them to acknowledge their feelings of pain and loss.

SYMPTOMS AND CAUSES OF MISCARRIAGES

At least four women approach the triage window each day in a state of total panic. They know they are pregnant and they are suffering from severe cramping and vaginal bleeding. Some are spotting lightly, while others are bleeding heavily and passing clots.

During the triage exam, women are asked how far along they are in their pregnancies. If they are less than fourteen weeks, there is little that can be done to stop the miscarriage from taking place. It is out of our hands and up to a "higher power" at that point.

In most cases the specific cause of a miscarriage is never determined. In about fifty percent of all cases, genetic abnormalities are found when the tissues are tested. A weak cervix can account for another ten to fifteen percent. Other causes may be due to a lack of adequate progesterone or androgen imbalances caused by autoimmune diseases, infections of chickenpox, rubella (measles), fever and chlamydia take their toll as well. One controversial theory suggests that a miscarriage is an immune response in which the mother's body rejects the father's genetic material.

Lifestyle factors also may play a significant role. Three cups of coffee or three hundred milligrams of any other caffeine can be problematic. Cocaine, crack use, environmental poisoning or exposure to radiation, will increase the risk of miscarriage. Emotional stress is also considered a possible factor.

Vaginal bleeding is usually, but not always, an early warning sign of an impending miscarriage. It is important to note that about twenty percent of all pregnant women have some bleeding during the first twelve weeks but less than half of them miscarry. I have witnessed many false alarms. Of course, these mothers-to-be panic and expect the worst.

An ultrasound is used to hear the presence of a fetal heartbeat. It also shows if the amniotic sac, which surrounds the fetus, is normal. The ultrasound can determine if the pregnancy is ectopic. This occurs when the fertilized egg attaches itself somewhere outside of the uterus, usually in the fallopian tubes. The fetus cannot survive outside the uterus and this condition can be fatal to a woman as it can lead to uncontrolled bleeding. The pregnancy must be ended immediately and the fetus is removed surgically.

After a miscarriage, blood is drawn to measure the hormone levels and the extent of the blood loss. The patient is checked for signs and symptoms of infection. A pelvic exam is performed to look for signs of changes in the cervix , ruptured membranes, and any remaining fetal tissue. If the pregnancy is more than fourteen weeks along, the doctor may recommend restricting physical activity, abstaining from sexual intercourse, even bed rest in some cases, until all the symptoms have ceased.

It is important to be as healthy as possible before conceiving. Plan ahead to treat any conditions that may cause a problem. Eat a healthy diet, get regular exercise, and sleep seven to eight hours a night. Discuss a vitamin regime with your healthcare provider. Manage stress levels. Don't smoke, abstain from alcohol and drink two cups or less of coffee per day. Avoid sports carrying a high risk for injury and always wear a seat belt. Check with the doctor BEFORE taking any medications, including over-the-counter products during pregnancy. Avoid x-rays, radiation, and contact with those with infectious diseases. These steps will help improve chances for an uncomplicated pregnancy and the birth of healthy baby.

11

CALL BACKS

One of my daily responsibilities is to call back ten patients who were treated in the emergency department within the previous two weeks. I inquire as to how they are feeling now and how they felt about the care that they received. Many patients are thrilled to have someone else to talk to about their health. Others are short with me and demand to know who I am and why am I calling them.

Reaching ten people at home can take an hour. Most times, however, it is a two-hour process because of answering machines and incorrect telephone numbers.

This particular evening I called a local number and asked for Marie. She had been treated for an eye infection and was diagnosed with a sty in her left eye.

Her mother answered and when I asked for Marie, I could hear the change in her voice. "Marie is sleeping right now and can't talk. This is Mary, her mother. Can I help you?" She sounded very upset. I introduced myself and told her why I was calling. "How is Marie feeling since her visit to the emergency last week? Is her eye healed?"

There was a moment of silence. Then I heard her voice crack with emotion and it was difficult for her to speak. She sounded devastated. "Marie doesn't have a sty. Your doctor referred her to Shearing Eye Clinic." She stammered, but continued, needing to vent. "They've put her through many tests and are doing cultures. No one can figure out what is wrong but Marie is now blind in one eye and can barely see out of the other one. What am I going to do? My daughter is only twenty-four years old and has two children, ages two and four. Her husband left her four months ago and I only have a part-time job as an apartment manager. I come home every day to a total disaster. The kids know Mom is sick and they are running rampant every day. We can't afford a baby-sitter. I am so frightened for us all. Marie is in terrible pain and now has a urinary tract infection and tonsillitis too. She has a fever of 102 and the medications are doing no good."

I was totally taken aback. I listened and told her how sorry I was. Mary sighed, grateful that someone was willing to listen to her. She then proceeded to tell me about how horribly Marie had been treated at the local welfare and social security offices. "I was a single-mom myself and never asked anyone for anything," she pleaded. "How can people be so cruel?" They keep asking for more forms and letters from various doctors. This could take months. What are we to do?" She added that Marie felt humiliated to be in such dire need and was upset over the perceived cruelty and indifference shown her.

I kept asking more questions and listening to her story. I identified with her pain and upset and imagined myself in her predicament. What a nightmare.

"Will Marie be able to see again once the infection is cleared up?" I asked hopefully. "No one knows at this point because they have no idea what's wrong with her." She lamented. I let her vent for a while longer. Certainly, she could not share her fears with Marie or the children; Mary needed to keep up a brave front for everyone concerned. It was taking its toll on her emotional well-being. I thought of Marie; blind, helpless,

12

BLESSINGS FROM HEAVEN?

One morning I peeked behind the curtain to room ten and saw a young woman, about twenty-five years old, sitting up in bed. She had a round baby face and long blonde hair. We made instant eye contact and she smiled and asked me to come in. Her name was Michele and she had an amazing story to tell me.

Michele had been diagnosed with a stomach tumor two years earlier. It had been surgically removed and after a short recovery, Michele returned to college to resume her life. Within two months, the tumor returned, causing more pain and medical problems. Her fears made her paralyzed to do anything about it. Michele's apprehension became a death wish. She withdrew from her friends and family and only communicated with them through the Internet.

Michele quit college and struggled to maintain a part-time

job in a fast food restaurant. She spent her free time at her computer, writing sonnets about her situation and her feelings of desperation. She contemplated suicide, but decided to let the tumor grow with the hope that it would kill her soon.

As she relayed her situation to me, I glanced down at her belly. The tumor was huge. She looked as though she had swallowed a cantaloupe. I was amazed at the sight. As she continued speaking, I was astounded by what had finally motivated her to seek treatment.

Michele spoke of the miracle that had happened to her. Kristen, her best friend, had sent her an e-mail encouraging Michele to submit her favorite poem to compete in an on-line poetry contest. The first place prize was $50,000 and a luncheon with some of the top writers in America. It took some persuasion, but Kristen succeeded in getting Michele to e-mail her best poem to the contest headquarters.

Out of twenty-five thousand entries, Michele's poem won the top prize. As she recounted this event, her entire face radiated. Winning the contest had rekindled her will to live. I felt her excitement and my body tingled.

Michele had attended the banquet two weeks before coming to the emergency room. During lunch, many of the participants took the microphone and praised her talents. She received a trophy, the $50,000 prize money, and found the entire experience thrilling beyond her wildest dreams.

A week after winning the award, Michele received an offer to write a song for an Academy award-winning director. Her hands trembled while she opened the envelope to show me the letter. She was beaming with pride and enthusiasm. Michele desperately wanted to live and she was terrified that she might have waited too long for medical intervention.

She came in through the emergency department and was admitted for more tests and more surgery. She was no longer afraid of the pain and discomfort. She wanted her health back more than anything in the world. I have to admit that I was also concerned about her condition. I found myself sending a prayer to my own higher power for her quick and full recovery.

We only spoke once during her five-hour stay in the emergency room, but I will never forget her. I hope to see her name when the credits roll at the end of the movie she told me about. I will definitely buy a copy of her song. Michele's case reminded me of the importance of taking good care of ourselves. No one knows what wonderful things await us in the future. We need to live each day as though something stupendous is right around the corner. Being so ill a few years back changed my own view of mortality and Michele jolted that memory. She sparked a renewed sense of urgency in me and I try to live every day to the fullest.

A CHRISTMAS GIFT

Christmas was insanely busy from start to finish. I thought I was thoroughly used up when I passed by room twelve. Out of the corner of my eye, I spotted a tiny, frail woman lying in bed, breathing through an oxygen mask. I felt an instant attraction so I walked over to find out why. She said her name was Annabelle and she was 101 years old. She was very alert and wanted to talk. I liked her immediately and wanted to know all about her life. I held her hand as I listened intently to her story.

Annabelle was born on a small farm in Tennessee. She was the eldest of nine children and the family was quite poor.

At sixteen, Annabelle met the love of her life. She and Edward were married the day she turned seventeen. They traveled throughout the south searching for employment. Times were very hard for them. Edward was called to military service during World War One and she was left alone to raise three small children. She became an expert seamstress and was awarded a contract to make uniforms for the soldiers from her state. Edward returned and life was good until he was again called to military service. This time it was World War Two. They were separated for four more years. Her children were now grown so she went to work at the local hospital as a nurse's aid. She also continued making uniforms and volunteered at the shelter to help prepare and pass out food to the destitute and the injured.

Annabelle spoke in a whisper and I had to strain to hear her but I was enthralled, none-the-less. Edward had died two decades earlier from heart failure and her children and all her siblings were now deceased. She had been living in a nursing home for the past eight years and she claimed she was treated with kindness and respect.

A half hour passed when Annabelle told me that she was ready to join her loved ones in heaven and asked if I could help her accomplish this last desire. I said "I can't do anything to medically intervene but I would be honored to assist you with my words. Are you certain that you really want to leave now?" I asked. She nodded yes so I told her to take some deep breaths and to gently close her eyes. She did so immediately. I let go of her hand and gently placed it back under the sheet so she would be more comfortable. I began to speak to her in a very quiet tone. I told her to relax her body; I began at her feet and suggested that she imagine a slight tingling sensation as her muscles let go of all the stress and discomfort in them. Once we made it to the top of her head, I took her on a visual life review. I restated all she had told me about her past journey, embellishing where I thought appropriate.

She never reopened her eyes. I made it all the way to the birth of her last great-great granddaughter when I noticed that her breathing, blood pressure, and pulse were slowing way down. I didn't want to disturb her dreams to confirm my suspicions but she seemed to be unconscious so I got up and quietly left her room. It was no longer Christmas and it was time for me to go home. I walked out the door with tears in my eyes. She had touched my spirit deeply and had given me a wonderful gift. Annabelle died ten minutes after I left her side.

13

DEATH –

THE FINAL FRONTIER (or is it?)

About three times a week, a "911" numeric message is displayed on my pager. I know that means someone is dying and I am needed in the treatment area immediately. My pulse quickens as I rush to one of the examination rooms to be part of the medical team who are scrambling to provide treatment. To an outsider, the scene appears chaotic, but this is not the case. The staff form an instant bond with only one mission; save that life. Usually present are several nurses, one doctor, two paramedics, a respiratory therapist and me. The adrenaline is pumping and I become focused and hyper-alert to everything I am witnessing.

In a loud voice, to be heard above all the shouting, I ask, "Are there any family or friends in the waiting room?" If the answer is yes, I then ask the team "Do you think the patient will survive the next few minutes? Does he (or she) have a chance to make it or should I begin the grieving process with the loved ones?"

There is rarely a predictable outcome and miracles do occur. Call it a higher power or fate but sometimes something intervenes to snatch the person back from brink of death. Not knowing what the end result will be, I struggle to maintain a balance between suggesting hope and prayer and beginning the grieving process. I try not to offer a false sense of encouragement if none exists.

I meet with those in the waiting room as soon as I get as much information as possible. This may be the worst time of their lives and I need to take control to be effective. I can usually spot those yearning for hope as soon as I enter the waiting area. Their faces are filled with fear and shock. Just my presence will turn their waking nightmare into stark reality.

I introduce myself and escort them to the Quiet Room where they can wait in a "safe space" to digest all that is happening in their world right now. It is horribly overwhelming when the finality of death is a real possibility, especially if it results from a sudden unexpected event.

A thousand thoughts rush through my head as I lead the way to the designated waiting area. The Quiet Room is located a short distance from where their loved one is fighting for their life.

At this point, most people are either totally distraught or in denial. My immediate goal is to help them remain calm. I always ask them about the circumstances that brought the patient to the hospital. I reassure them that the doctors are doing everything possible. I tell them that the patient is very critical and anything can happen. When I already know the outcome, it is difficult to sit there and pretend that their prayers will be answered. Fear fills the room. I help by asking about the family dynamics and the patient's medical history. If I know that the patient didn't make it, my stomach churns while I ask questions about the deceased. They often profess their dreams of the future and what they will do differently if it all turns out well. Most wrap themselves in feelings of guilt, anger, or blame for the immediate crisis. I listen attentively as this is an opportunity for them to vent without being judged or condemned. I try to keep the conversation focused on the past or the present. The future is too tentative and too frightening to consider right now.

It can seem like an eternity waiting for the doctor to arrive with some news. If the patient died, the doctor explains what happened and states his best guess as to the cause. The doctor only stays for a few minutes. After taking his exit, I take over and reiterate what was said to them. I try to translate the words into layman's terms so they understand what happened. A mental bomb explodes in the room. Sometimes the result is instant, heart-wrenching pain and sorrow. Shock sets in rapidly and it takes a few minutes to fully comprehend what just occurred. Some people begin to sweat profusely, others will vomit. Many try to intellectualize the situation. I listen to their words of pain until an unsettling calm results. I tell them how sorry I am that this has happened to them. Once everyone has settled down enough to listen, I ask if they have ever discussed how the patient wanted their death to be handled. Did they want to be buried or cremated? When the time seems right, I inquire about organ donation knowing that I am asking them to adjust to so much turmoil in a short period of time.

Depending on the condition of the deceased, one body can help make a better life for many others. Heart transplants are used for those with inoperable heart failure. Eyes can help two blind people to see again. Kidneys can allow two people to live productive lives without having to be sustained by dialysis. Skin is used to help burn victims, veins are extracted for heart surgeries and some bones can assist others to walk again or repair a severely injured arm or leg so it can again be functional. Livers can prolong life for those suffering from end-stage liver disease and pancreas can help those suffering the effects of diabetes.

If this patient becomes an organ donor, I call the representative from the local donor center to come to the hospital. They will explain the procedures in more detail and obtain written authorization from the closest remaining relative. It is important that the family feel positive about their decision to donate. Nothing is done without full disclosure of the methods and procedures involved.

As an organ donor, the body is kept in a functioning state by mechanical devices such as a ventilator until it is taken to surgery. If there is to an open casket during the funeral service, the mortician will leave only the head and hands exposed and the eye lids are sewn shut. The deceased appears to be asleep. Donation can ease the pain of the death for the family. Some good will come out of their tremendous loss and it can provide life to so many others.

If the survivors want additional time with the patient, the nurse brings the body to the viewing room on a gurney. Most people need to see their loved one again. The body is covered with a sheet, leaving the head and one arm exposed. This provides those grieving with a part of their loved one to touch for one last time.

The viewing is a crucial part of making the preceding death a reality. They saw this person alive just a short while ago. Though told of the death, I believe that it is important that they see and touch the body so the grieving process can begin. The length of viewing time varies. Some people only stay a minute and run out sobbing. Others take longer to say their "good-bye's." I usually remain with them during this process and often I am the first one to touch the body. It helps them to do the same.

During the first few months, this was the most difficult part of my job. Now I look forward to helping the survivors get through this crucial period. My eyes fill up every time I am present for the gut-wrenching reality test. I help them place telephone calls to family members not present and we work out the details of how they will dispose of the body.

After the initial phase is completed, I stand up so they know that it is time for them to leave the hospital. This moment is heart-breaking for me. It has been a horrific experience for the survivors and they are leaving the hospital without their loved one. Their prayers went unanswered and their lives have been changed forever.

SUDDEN DEATH

Abe arrived by ambulance one Sunday afternoon. He had collapsed while jogging in a nearby park with his wife. This run was like any other until the last lap. Nina, his wife, witnessed him grab his chest and fall to the ground. A stranger rushed over and began CPR while Nina scrambled through her purse for her cell phone to place a frantic call to 911. The ambulance was there in a matter of minutes but Abe never regained consciousness. The sirens could be heard inside the hospital and the staff had been notified that the paramedics were on their way. Everyone was ready to administer life-saving procedures the moment he arrived.

The ambulance screeched up to the entrance and the medics scrambled to get the patient to us as quickly as possible. I was informed that his wife had ridden in the ambulance with her husband and was waiting for me outside. I found her and escorted her to the Quiet Room. Her disbelief was immediately apparent. "This is impossible," she proclaimed with a mixture of assurance and fear. "Abe is in perfect health. The doctor just said so a few weeks ago." I hear this often. Abe was fifty-four and had a complete physical two months earlier. The test showed no discernible medical problems and he was given a clean bill of health. Abe was a staunch believer in physical fitness and he consumed vitamins and herbal supplements on a daily basis He also worked out in the gym and ran five miles every other day.

"I am very sorry that this happened but it sounds like he suffered a heart attack." I was trying to both comfort and speak truthfully to Nina as I continued, "Often the tests used for a general physical do not include checking the arteries of the heart so unless he had high blood pressure, chest pains or shortness of breath, the problem would not show up. I realize that this has caught you totally by surprise and I am sorry for that but it does not change the situation." I paused for a moment to give her time to comprehend what I was saying. For twenty minutes Nina tried to dispute the facts and she continued to deny the reality of the situation. Finally, Dr. Green arrived to deliver the news that Abe had suffered a massive heart attack and had probably died before he hit he ground. He tried to be consoling by adding that because of the suddenness of the attack, Abe probably felt no pain. Nina was so stunned that she couldn't argue with the doctor. She was in shock for about five minutes before she started to weep.

I stayed with Nina for the next thirty minutes until Abe's

body was brought to the viewing room. I asked if she was ready to see him and Nina assured me that she was. This was the first time I had seen Abe and I, too, was surprised that he had died of a sudden heart attack. He was a strapping man with well-developed muscles. His hair was blonde, short, and wispy. It fell onto his forehead in a way that gave him a very boyish look. He was clean-shaven and other than a few smile lines around his eyes, appeared much younger than fifty-four.

The viewing room is very small and bland with white walls. There are no pictures, phones or chairs. I stood on one side of Abe and Nina stood on the other. She continued talking to me about their relationship and all of their activities without acknowledging that Abe's body was on a gurney between us. Many times I attempted to escort Nina out of the viewing room to the Quiet Room to talk further but each time she adamantly refused. She wanted to stay with Abe as long as possible. She was not accepting Abe's death.

We spoke for hours and I learned that Abe had spent eight years in prison for an armed robbery he committed while living in Georgia. He had survived two serious stabbings and four years of bad institutional food. While serving his sentence, he had spent most of his time weight training. I saw the stretch marks inside his upper arms, clear indications that he pressed more weight than his body could handle adequately.

Abe had been paroled five months before his death and he had become a health fanatic in a frantic attempt to correct years of damage from drugs, alcohol and incarceration. Nina had waited for him, never dating anyone else during those years away from him. She was not ready to let go after such a short "honeymoon."

I was uncomfortable spending so much time with a corpse. Medical personnel spend time treating the patient during the code. This may continue for an hour or more. Once the time of death is declared , everyone but the main nurse leaves the room. She disconnects much of the tubing from the body and puts away the equipment and tools that were left laying around. This may take five minutes. Even morticians spend only a limited amount of time preparing the body for viewing and burial or cremation.

That day, Nina and I spent three hours standing beside

Abe's decomposing body while Nina clung firmly to her denial. Even while holding his hand, she protested the reality of his death. "He is still warm," she said "Are you sure that he's dead?" "Yes." I firmly told her. "The body loses about one degree of heat per hour." Abe had only been dead about two hours at this point. I understood her reluctance to admit the truth and I remained calm but at the same time I gently tried to get her to focus on the reality of the situation and her future plans.

The coroner was notified and he wanted to meet with Nina because Abe was young and his death was sudden. Those two facts triggered an investigation so the coroner could rule out murder as cause of death. He arrived four hours later and asked Nina many questions about the preceding events of the day. He asked about Abe's health, their relationship and their financial situation. Nina passed the test and signed the official papers. She decided to have Abe's body cremated and we left the quiet room. I escorted her out to the car and she reached out and hugged me. I was relieved to finally have this ordeal over with. I headed back to the ER for my next assignment.

Four hours later I received a call from Nina. She was

adamant that the cause of Abe's death was either the vitamins or the herbal supplement he had begun taking a few weeks before his death. She demanded an autopsy to prove her theory. Abe had no medical insurance and an autopsy costs $6,000 or more. I knew she didn't have much money. She could not possibly afford it and the hospital would demand payment in advance. She then wanted his blood tested, but no blood samples were taken from Abe because he was already dead when he arrived. She was enraged and was determined to prove her theory. I explained that her anger was a normal part of the grief process and that she needed to let go of the reasons for Abe's death. She needed to begin to accept his death and start to focus on herself.

She had already told me that they had no savings and she needed to find a job right away to support herself. I asked if she had any family support available. "Yes." she replied. "My daughter lives in Lake Tahoe and she is coming down tomorrow to stay with me for a few days." She began to cry. I knew that Nina was starting to come to terms with the situation and she was struggling to cope with her grief. I was confident that over time, she would be able to go on with her life.

A few weeks after Abe's death, I was called to Station Two and was told that a visitor wanted to see me. I arrived to find Nina waiting at the desk. Her face lit up when she saw me. She ran over and gave me a warm, prolonged hug. I asked how she was doing. "Much better now," she exclaimed with a huge smile on her face. "I had to bring my daughter to the emergency room today for abdominal pains, so I wanted to find you and thank you for all of your help." She did look better and caught me up on the details of her life since that terrible day. "I got my old job back at the casino where I worked before Abe's parole. Did I tell you I was a cocktail waitress? I am doing much better now and having my daughter here really helps." I wished her well, gave her another hug, and left.

As I walked down the hall, I contemplated death and how it affects the living. With a prolonged illness, the person can make arrangements and everyone mentally begins to prepare. With an unexpected death, there is shock, disbelief, and denial. But as human beings, we persevere and people do adjust to this transition. I do my best to get them off to a good start.

BRAIN DEATH

A person is declared brain dead when there is no evidence of brain function. Unfortunately, this condition is irreversible. There are two specific tests that the physician can use to make this diagnosis. One of these tests is called a cerebral blood flow study which determines if there is blood flow to the brain. The other test is an electroencephalogram, also known as an EEG, which checks to verify whether any electrical brain activity remains. In lieu of these tests, the patient can be assessed for brain death by the absence of brain stem function. This is demonstrated by such things as the absence of pupil response, absence of gag reflex, lack of response to painful stimuli, and cessation of spontaneous respirations. The occurrence of all of these must not be related to any sedation.

Brain death usually occurs in one of two ways. The first is from total and complete arrest of heart and lung function. The second is from a total and irreversible cessation of brain functioning caused by a catastrophic injury to the brain which causes all neurological activity to stop. This can occur from events such as gunshot wounds, motor vehicle accidents, brain tumors, and brain bleeds, falls and physical assaults.

Many wonder why the heart continues to beat if the patient is brain dead. This is because the heart has a pacemaker of its own. One could actually remove the heart from the body, place it in a saline solution, give it oxygen, and it would continue to beat. The body functions exhibited are only sustained by machines. The death of the brain is the death of the person by all legal, medical, and ethical principals.

This is a devastating time for those left behind. I do my very best to help them to understand that there is no longer any hope for the survival of the person they know and love. The person is gone even if the body can function minimally by artificial means. It is the family's decision to allow the physician to "pull the plug," in other words to stop all artificial means of keeping the organs functioning.

This is an extremely difficult situation and I have to ask my next question carefully and with tremendous sensitivity. "Do you know if your loved one wished to donate his organs to save others?" Once brain death occurs, time is a factor if the doctors are to harvest the organs successfully for transplantation.

14

ORGAN DONATION

"Anyone Can Be A Hero"

Organ donation can offer a better quality of life or even life itself to another person. It is an opportunity for the family to make the death less painful by helping others to live. The need for organs far exceeds the available supply. Thousands of men, women and children die every year while waiting for organs. According to The Living Bank, a non-profit organization devoted to tissue and organ donation, a new name is added to this list of sixty thousand every thirteen minutes. Every day sixteen people die waiting for that organ that never comes. An average of sixty-three transplants are performed daily. One donor can save many and enhance the lives of up to one hundred recipients.

All states offer donor registration cards at the Departments of Motor Vehicles but that is not all that should be done. It is important to discuss your thoughts with family members so that they are aware of your desire to contribute. This also prevents any confusion or uncertainty later if an emergency situation arises where death is imminent. A spouse or someone close should sign as a witness on the donor card. Share this decision with the primary physician and your spiritual advisor. Carry the card with you at all times. More importantly, encourage others to become donors. Most religions of the world support organ and tissue donation. It is considered a compassionate thing to do. Personally, I think it is the greatest gift one could ever bequeath.

Many people fear that the medical treatment will be inferior if it is known that they are planning to be organ donors. This is totally false. There are safeguards in place and a consensus must be reached before death is declared. Recovery of organs is only done AFTER all life-saving measures have been exhausted and permission is granted.

If the family agrees to the donation, I place a call to our local donor agency and a representative arrives at the hospital to go over the laws and the procedures. The donor's family incurs no expense, nor do they receive any compensation. The organ procurement program or transplant center pays for everything related to the procedures.

The physicians that treat the living do not work with organ donation. It is a team of specialized surgeons who will be extracting the organs and tissues. There is no financial benefit to the treating physicians.

For those who don't believe in cremation, the body is treated with total respect during the procedures and is not disfigured. The funeral is not delayed and an open casket may still be presented for viewing during the funeral service.

For further information on organ donation, contact The Living Bank, 4545 Post Oak Place, Suite 315, Houston, Texas, 77027. You can also call them at (800) 528-2971. Their web site is www.livingbank.org.

15

CRISIS IN HEALTH CARE

Providing adequate and timely medical care has become an overwhelming problem in this country today. While the need for health care professionals is exploding along with the population growth, only a small percentage of new arrivals to Las Vegas are employed in the health care system. Nevada has the lowest ratio of nurses to patients of any state in America today. As of 2002, the state of Nevada is also suffering from a malpractice insurance crisis. This is forcing many health professionals to retreat to less expensive states in record numbers, further adding to the shortage. The university system is facing the possibility of closing its medical school. Everyone employed in the health care delivery system is very worried about the future and our fears are justified. Las Vegas is leading the way in this crisis. Surely this trend will repeat itself throughout the country.

We all must be concerned and if the issues are not addressed adequately, and soon, medical care will change for the worse. It is inevitable that we will all face health problems and crisis situations. After all, we are only human and our bodies are not designed to last forever. Every one of us will need tune-ups to keep going. Most of us are unaware of what is taking place in the health care field until we actually need help. It is on the news daily yet many patients are shocked and dismayed at the long waiting periods and the shortage of doctors and nurses to care for them.

The system is imploding for a number of reasons. All medical facilities receiving federal funding are required, by law, to give medical assistance to those claiming a need. With or without medical insurance, everyone is treated equally in the emergency room. The medical facility I work for is also mandated by law to admit anyone picked up for public intoxication. On any given day, up to twenty-five percent of our treatment rooms are occupied by people "under the influence" of drugs and alcohol sleeping it off to the cost of one thousand dollars and more, per visit. Add another six hundred to eight hundred dollars if they arrive by ambulance (which is often the case), and you can see just how quickly our health-care system can self-destruct. Our country is severely lacking in providing psychiatric services and drug and alcohol treatment programs to those in need.

In Las Vegas, the police bring the mentally ill and the publicly intoxicated to the local hospitals for basic care and warehousing until a bed becomes available in one of the few treatment centers set up to deal with their problems.

Add to those numbers, the patients who come to the emergency room for sore throats, ingrown toe nails, menstrual cramps, colds, low fevers and stomach aches and it should be no surprise that the waiting time to see a physician in the emergency room can be anywhere from two to twelve hours.

Yet, the staff must keep everyone calm, provide medical treatment and maintain a sense of professionalism despite overwhelming circumstances.

The average age of a nurse in America is forty-six and new recruits are not picking up the slack. If changes aren't implemented soon, we will all be in serious trouble when we need help.

REDUCING THE MEDICAL CARE CRISIS

The future of emergency medical care in America is in a perilous state. There are many things each one of us can do to help alleviate this situation.

We must take better care of ourselves through a healthy diet, annual check-ups and regular exercise. Believe it or not, even washing your hands more often throughout the day, especially after elimination, will improve your health. Be proactive. Take advantage of all of the resources available. There are many web sites on line that provide quality information, but know your source before you consider it reliable. Read books and magazine articles and watch informative television programs. If you feel that something is not "right" physically , have your physician or clinic check you out.

Do not wait until the pain is unbearable to go to the emergency room. You may need to wait hours to be seen by a physician and no pain medication can be administered to you before that occurs.

If the problem is chronic, get a referral from your general practitioner for a specialist. For minor aches and pains, try a physical therapist or a chiropractor. Acupuncture, acupressure and massage therapists may be able to help, too. Keep ice and heat packs at home and find out what kinds of exercises can be beneficial, and do them. An emergency room doctor can only administer drugs that will temporarily relieve the pain. Think about it—Do you really want to wait six to twelve hours for treatment to then be disappointed that you are not magically healed?

There are other services that should be addressed by a doctor or clinic Pregnancy tests, minor scrapes and sprains, bladder infections, minor headaches and stomach ailments are not appropriate reasons to seek medical attention in an emergency setting. One young woman came in for a pimple on her forehead. She took up valuable time and resources that were desperately needed elsewhere.

Another crisis in the emergency room is the homeless and/or drug and alcohol -addicted looking for a free place to "crash" for the night. Hospitals employ a limited number of personnel to handle emergencies. They are not there to treat alcoholism, drug addiction and other societal problems.

As a professional in the medical field, I can attest to the fact that we, as a society, need to improve how we treat the mentally ill and addicted. When Ronald Reagan was governor of California, he closed most of the mental hospitals. The remaining states followed his lead as a way to save money, creating many of our problems today. More community treatment centers and resources are needed for those suffering from addiction and mental illness. This is essential if we are to reduce the burden on our hospitals.

Don't abuse the ambulance system. Paramedics are there to sustain life until further intervention can be provided. The system is not designed to perform taxi functions and should not be used in non-emergency situations. Many abuse the ambulance services because they believe they will be seen and treated faster than coming in by car or foot. Unfortunately, they are correct. In Nevada, the paramedic remains with his/ her patient until a hospital room is made available. Patients are often taken ahead of others more needy because the paramedics must be available to assist the next person calling in for help. The backlog causes delays in reaching those in life-threatening situations. Abusing ambulance services may cause a delay that can result in the death of someone in dire need of intervention.

The system is completely overburdened and it is beginning to fall apart. Doctors and nurses are leaving their chosen fields in record numbers. "Burn out" is happening even to those just beginning their careers. Health care workers have tremendous responsibilities and they are all being overworked. Meal breaks are a rarity. Who among us is capable of working their hardest for twelve hours without any breaks? This can lead to oversights and errors. The average age for a nurse is forty six and they will be retiring en masse within the next two decades, just when the baby boomers will need them the most. Doctors are leaving states with skyrocketing medical malpractice premiums for states with more reasonable rates. Many are retiring early or choosing other occupations to avoid the threat of lawsuits.

Encourage your children to become health care workers. We will desperately need them to care for us in the near future.

More than one hundred and seventy thousand people have moved to Las Vegas since I began this job. The local hospitals are currently struggling to function with about half the number of staff needed to adequately treat our bulging population. Each week, emergency room patients wait longer to get a bed and receive treatment. Patients resent the long wait times and they are becoming angry and hostile to the those trying to provide care. The staff members feel the pressure and often react with indifference and bad attitudes. Many of us will die because resources and assistance are in such short supply.

HOW TO TRIGGER MIRACLES

Miracles happen frequently in the emergency room. We are all capable of creating them. Sometimes it begins when a friend, loved one, or even a by-stander, convinces another to seek medical treatment. They are often the ones who call for an ambulance or drive the individual to the hospital. I meet them every day. The sick person may be in denial and rationalize that their problem is minor and will simply "go away". Often a "simple" problem turns out to be a major life-threatening event that may have resulted in death if not treated immediately.

Our thoughts and fears can be our worst enemies. Fear stops many from seeking help. Your actions and persistence can save lives. Gently ask why they are afraid to get help and allow them to share their feelings Once you know what the issues are, acknowledge them and be sympathetic. Be supportive and encouraging but persistent. Refuse to take "no" for an answer. Offer to call for an ambulance. If there is time and the situation is not critical, drive them to the hospital. Keep them company while they wait. Going to a hospital for treatment can be a frightening experience. The general public associates hospitals with pain and death and no-one wants to be there alone. Be pro-active. Let your instincts be your guide. So what if they get angry at you for "forcing them." You can take it and be proud of yourself for doing the right thing. Every day at least one patient tells me about all the warning signs they ignored. They were hoping that the symptoms would just disappear. We can only treat those who get to us in time. We truly are "our brother's keeper." Some day someone may do the same for you.

Become a volunteer at your local hospital or nursing home. Staff are in short supply and we need all the assistance we can get.

At all times, be sure to carry a list of emergency telephone numbers and a list of all your current medications and dosages.

While still healthy and capable, decide if you want to be on life support in the event that a tragic situation arises. Your desires must be in writing. If you do not have the official documents filled out and signed beforehand, the doctors must do everything possible to prolong your life, regardless of the quality, or lack thereof.

Sign up to become an organ and tissue donor. Your death can mean a new start at life for many. Share your desire with your loved ones so they are not forced to make that decision in the midst of their grief and sorrow.

Last but not least, take good care of yourself every day. If you are experiencing pains or ailments that concern you, seek medical advice early on. If you don't understand what your doctor tells you, ask again or find another doctor you can develop a positive relationship with.

We are each given one "temple" and our essence lives in it from our birth until our death. Treasure it. There is nothing more valuable than your health and contrary to what we all want to believe, doctors can't "fix" every problem. It is up to us to treat ourselves with the utmost care and to act as our own physician and guardian.

16

EPILOGUE

Eighteen months have passed since I first walked through the doors to the hospital. With an increased sense of confidence and self-assurance, I have calmly handled all my cases. I have witnessed people in extreme states of pain. I have observed the doctors sewing up various body parts injured, bleeding and raw from every kind of accident imaginable. I can testify to many near-deaths and have spent innumerable hours with families and their deceased loved-ones. I was beginning to think that not much would rattle me anymore - I was wrong.

It was 10:00 on a Sunday night and I had worked four twelve-hour shifts in a row. I was feeling exhausted and uninspired when Nurse Cheryl informed me that a "code" was arriving momentarily by ambulance. The adrenaline began to pump inside all of us. The staff hustled to get the necessary drugs and equipment to room nine to prepare for the patient's arrival. Within moments, three paramedics and two firemen rushed in with a seventy-seven year old man on a gurney. Even before hearing their report, it was obvious that Mr. Greenberg was in big trouble with CPR being administered by one of the paramedics. The oxygen mask was in place over the man's nose and face. He was quickly moved from the temporary stretcher to one of our gurneys. Nurse Yolanda grabbed her scissors from the pocket of her smock and quickly cut off his clothing. Dr. Trapp barked out orders with incredible speed. IVs were inserted in both of the patient's arms. "Is the family here?" I yelled. "Yes, his wife and son are in the in the waiting room." one of the paramedics answered. "They followed the ambulance here."

I rushed to the waiting room to update them on the man's condition and to find out what happened before he collapsed. I did my best to assure them that the doctor was doing everything humanly possible to save his life but I also advised them that he was very unstable and the situation could go either way. I explained that I would be their liaison and I would keep them informed. Visitors are rarely allowed back to the treatment area during this critical time period. All available room is needed for the equipment and personnel to do their jobs as quickly and as efficiently as possible.

I spent the next hour watching and praying that Mr. Greenberg would survive. His blood pressure continued to drop. No one involved in his direct care dared to take a breath. The room became stifling; Everyone was totally focused on the mission at hand. Meanwhile, I continued to meet with the family every fifteen minutes. The loved ones waiting included his wife and eight other family members. They were all red-faced from crying and there was a feeling of panic amongst them all. I will never forget the fearful look on all of their faces every time they spotted me walking towards them. I encouraged them to pray to a higher power and comforted them as their vigil continued.

One time while I was in the treatment area watching the medical team, Mr. Greenburg flat lined which means that his heart stopped beating. "Step back!" yelled the doctor. "I am going to shock him." I was already emotionally involved with his family and I desperately wanted him to survive for their sake. Electric shocks were administered four times with no results. The fifth try barely brought him back from the dead. I began to breathe easier although I knew he had little chance of surviving what appeared to be a major heart attack.

I continued observing Mr. Greenberg in the treatment room and bonding with his family in the waiting room. I could tell that he was very well loved. I think I wanted him to live almost as much as they did. At one point, they were able to tell me what happened just before his heart attack.

Three short hours before he was admitted into the hospital, the family had returned from Los Angeles. They had traveled en mass to attend Mr. and Mrs. Greenberg's first granddaughter's wedding. Mr. Greenberg had danced the afternoon away. Everyone had a wonderful time reuniting with friends and family and celebrating the glorious event.

They had gotten home without any traffic problems and had just finished dinner when Mr. Greenberg walked outside into the garden. "Don't turn on the sprinkler." Mrs. G. had quipped to everyone, "Joe is upstairs taking a shower and the water may burn him." Five minutes later she walked outside and discovered Mr. G by the back door lying on the ground and unconscious. He did not appear to be breathing. She yelled for Joe to call 911 and she began CPR.

With a quivering voice she told me that she and her husband had been married for fifty-one years and they recently moved in with their oldest son, Joe. I was grateful she would be surrounded by family if her husband did not survive.

Mr. Greenberg's physical condition continued to deteriorate. His blood pressure was now in the low thirties and the drugs administered to stabilize him were no longer circulating throughout his body. Nothing seemed to help. Forty-five minutes later a cardiologist arrived to evaluate the EKG , the chest x-ray and the other test results. The doctor requested that I move the family to the Quiet Room so that she could update them on his condition.

After introductions, she began by telling them that Mr. Greenberg's heart had stopped. There was a gasp, an instant rush of fear, and the tears began to flow. "He is back now but it doesn't look good." she explained. "We think he has a blocked artery that may have caused his heart attack. We need to perform a procedure to open up that artery but it may not do any good. His brain is showing no activity right now and that is irreversible. If he does survive, he will be a vegetable." The family was flabbergasted and didn't know what to do. Should they allow the procedure or cut off life-support and let him go with dignity? The family turned to Mrs. G looking for the answer. But she was in shock and could barely utter a word.

At that moment, Mrs. Greenberg could not grasp the reality of the situation. I restated the doctor's position and reminded the family that their loved one was gone. I believed that his soul had already left his body. The bible describes the body as being the temple of the soul. Without a soul we are all merely skin, blood, and bones. The doctor exited the room for a few moments to give them time to decide. I suggested that they take a vote so that the responsibility for the decision could be shared equally. I gently reminded them that his body was now merely a shell, not the person they had known and loved. I also reminded them that if they opted for the procedure, he would most likely not survive; He would die on a sterile bed, away from them all. I promised them that if they authorized shutting off the life support equipment, I would take them into his room so they could be with him when he passed on. The family all agreed that the best thing to do was to stop life support.

Overcome with sadness and with tears in my eyes, I escorted them to his bedside. The machines were all disconnected and one by one, they took his hand, touched his face, looked into his glazed-over eyes, and said their good-byes. Another niece and nephew joined us in the crowded room and the air became heavy with sadness. We all remained at his bedside for about twenty minutes. When they were ready to leave I escorted them back to the Quiet Room to regroup and make some necessary final decisions.

I took this opportunity to try to refocus their attention on the events of the weekend. A few short hours ago they had been sitting in their dining room eating dinner and reliving their wonderful weekend. I spoke about grief and the need to take care of themselves and each other during this difficult period.

As we were heading for the door, I saw Dr. Datson. I told the family that he was the ER doctor who had given his all to save Mr. Greenberg. Immediately, the eldest son asked me to call him over so the family could express their appreciation. The doctor seemed somewhat taken aback and uncomfortable. What would they say to him? After all, wasn't this a "failed" case for him? Not to the Greenberg family. They shook his hand and thanked him profusely for doing the that best he could for their loved one. Both the doctor and I were moved by their gratitude

Before leaving the hospital, every one of them reached out and hugged me and thanked me for all my help. I wished that I could have done more. As I walked them to the exit I offered words of encouragement and compassion.

I walked back into the emergency room to inform the team about the patient's weekend and the happiness he had experienced on his last day of life. This helped the staff to let go of the cloud of death that was hanging over Station One. As I walked towards my office to sign out for the day, I heard the intercom come on. "Code 99, West 237. Code 99, West 237". I stopped in my tracks as if I had just run into a brick wall. At that moment I thought about the person I did not even know, fighting to stay alive for just a little while longer.

My shift was over and I was grateful to finally be on the road heading home. My heart was heavy. Today I experienced laughter and tears, pain and sorrow, loss and acceptance ... but I wouldn't have it any other way.

17

CONCLUSION

I earned a Master's degree in medical social work back in 1980. My first job out of graduate school was in the juvenile justice system working with convicted murderers, child molesters and rapists. Since then I have treated clients with all types of problems. For ten years I ran a private investigation business specializing in reuniting adoptees with birth relatives. During my "capitalistic phase" I worked as a financial planner and stockbroker but it took a severe personal medical crisis to bring me back to seeking my passion. Today the hepatitis C virus is still undetectable in my blood. I look and feel healthy and I continue to wake up every day grateful to be alive.

This part of my journey started out with tremendous anticipation and trepidation. I have never learned so much, so fast. I started out feeling intimidated by death, my own and others. Death does not have to be frightening and the pain of grief is tolerable; it does subside in time. Many people outlive their bodies usefulness while others pass way before their time. Sometimes some superior power intervenes and assists where all the finest doctors, medications, electric shocks and CPR fail.

I have gone through many personal changes during this past year and a half. My job description should include being able to access my heart and my soul. I have become keenly aware of the impact my words and actions had on others more vulnerable. I had to learn to filter out much of the emotional intensity in order to be effective. I also have had to become emotionally numb to the pain and suffering I encounter on a regular basis. I will forever be grateful that I have been given the opportunity to share so much of myself with others in their time of need. I can't think of any job that is more rewarding.

Please use the information provided in this book for problems that might affect you or someone you know. We can all receive excellent care if the system is used in the way it was intended.

My wish for you is that you enjoy a long and healthy life.

Sources and Resources

Death
Bolton, Iris, "My Son...My Son...A Guide To Healing After Death, Loss, Or Suicide" 1090 Crest Brook Lane, Roswell, Ga. 30075

Diabetes
WWW.msnbc.com/news/diabetes
WebMD.com
www.healthmsn.com
www.lifescan.com

Domestic Violence
Domestic Violence: "The Facts"- A Handbook to STOP Violence (Reprinted by permission of Battered Women Fighting Back, Boston, Ma (617) 482-9497
National Hotline: 1-800-799-SAFE

Health Care Crisis
Brophy, Mary "HealthCare's Perfect Storm"U.S. News World Report, July 1, 2002 pg. 39-40
Babula, Joelle Las Vegas Review -Journal February 19, 2002 "Health Care: Nurses Woes"
Robert Wood Johnson Foundation "The American Nursing Shortage"
www.rwf.org/news
"America speaks On The Health Care Liability Crisis"
www.hcla.org
'Health Care Crisis: Who's At Risk?"
www.pbs.org/healthcarecrisis/

Heart Disease
National Cholesterol Education Program, Cardiovascular Disease
www.MedicineNet.com Heart Attacks
Women and Heart Disease, Karen Arcotta, MD. F.A.C.C. University of Nevada School of Medicine, Las Vegas

Hepatitis C
Everson, Gregory T. MD. and Weinburg, Hedy, "Living With Hepatitis C, A Survivor's Guide." 1999
www.hepatitis.com

Homeless
Martha Burt and Barbara Cohen, "America's Homeless Numbers, Characteristics and Programs That Save Them" Urban Institute, 2100 M. St. N.W. Washington, D.C. 20037
Interagency Council On The Homeless, U.S. Dept. Of Housing and Development Community Connections, PO Box 7189, Gaithersburg, MD 20898

Kidney Stones
WebMD Health Kidney Stones in Adults http://my.webmd.com/content/article
American Foundation for Urological Disease, 300 west Pratt Street Baltimore, MD 21201-2463
(800) 242-2383
National Kidney Foundation, 30 East 33rd St, New York, New York 10016 (800) 622-9010

Miscarriages
www.deanandroy.com
www.ivf.com/misc.html
www.incid.org/misman/.html

Organ Donation
The Living Bank, PO Box 6725
Houston, TX 77265
1-800-528-2971
www.livingbank.org
Nevada Donor Network, Inc.
2085 E. Sahara Avenue, Las Vegas, Nevada 89104
796-9600

<u>Miscellaneous Web Sites For Medical Information</u>

www.webmd.com
www.mayoclinic.com
www.johnshopkins.com
www.ucsf.com
www.ucla.com
www.health.msn.com
www.hepatitis.com

ORDER FORM

❐ Yes, I want _____ copies of Temple of the Soul at $12.95 each, plus shipping/handling per book. (Nevada residents please add 7.5% sales tax per book). All orders must be paid in U.S. funds.

Shipping/handling charges:

Up to $50.00	$5.00
$51.00 to $100.00	$10.00
$101.00 to $150.00	$15.00
$151.00 to $240.00	$20.00

❐ My check or money order for $_____ is enclosed.
❐ Mastercard Number_____
❐ Expiration Date_____
❐ Visa Number_____
❐ Expiration Date_____

Name_____

Company_____

Address_____

City_____

State/Province_____Zip Code_____

Phone_____Fax_____

Email_____

Signature_____

Please make check or money order payable to:

Marsha Oritt
2800 Autumn Haze Lane
Las Vegas, NV 89117-0633
Fax: 702-804-0569

Thank you for your order!